The Lucky Ones

OUR STORIES OF ADOPTING CHILDREN FROM CHINA

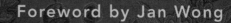
Foreword by Jan Wong

the Lucky Ones

OUR STORIES OF ADOPTING CHILDREN FROM CHINA

Edited by Ann Rauhala

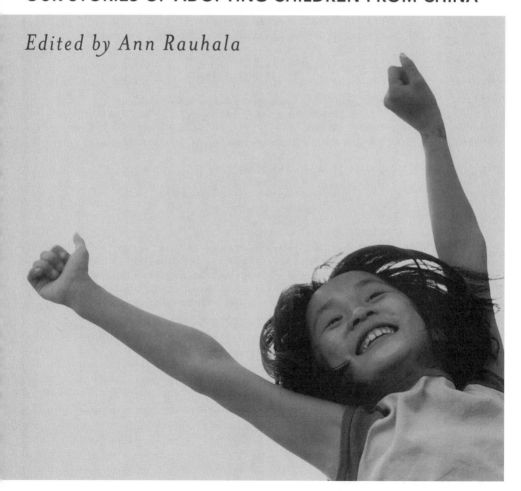

Published by ECW PRESS
2120 Queen Street East, Suite 200, Toronto, Ontario, Canada M4E 1E2

LIBRARY AND ARCHIVES OF CANADA CATALOGUING IN PUBLICATION

Rauhala, Ann
The lucky ones: Our stories of adopting children from China / Ann Rauhala.

ISBN-13: 978-1-55022-823-6
ISBN-10: 1-55022-823-4

1. Adoptive parents—Biography. 2. Adopted children—China.
3. Intercountry adoption. 4. Interracial adoption. I. Rauhala, Ann

HV875.5.L82 2008   362.7340951   C2007-907093-0

Editor: Jen Hale
Cover Design: David Gee
Text Design and Typesetting: Melissa Kaita
Cover photo: Catherine Farquharson
Printing: Transcontinental

The publication of The Lucky Ones *has been generously supported by the Canada Council for the Arts which last year invested $20.1 million in writing and publishing throughout Canada, by the Ontario Arts Council, by the Government of Ontario through Ontario Book Publishing Tax Credit, by the OMDC Book Fund, an initiative of the Ontario Media Development Corporation, and by the Government of Canada through the Book Publishing Industry Development Program (BPIDP).*

Canada Council Conseil des Arts   ONTARIO ARTS COUNCIL
for the Arts   du Canada   CONSEIL DES ARTS DE L'ONTARIO

Distribution
Canada: Jaguar Book Group, 100 Armstrong Avenue, Georgetown, Ontario, L7G 5S4
United States: IPG, 814 North Franklin Street, Chicago, Illinois 60610

PRINTED AND BOUND IN CANADA

ECW PRESS
ecwpress.com

For all our children and for the ones left behind

Contents

Preface

MAKE NO MISTAKE. The mothers and fathers of children from China know that *we're* the lucky ones,

We hear that adjective "lucky" foisted on our children at the airport, the grocery store, the toddlers' playgroup. The curious stranger approaches with a knowing look, assessing our little Asian peach peering up from under the fuzzy hat.

The comments start, often without much thought about the child who is listening. Yes, China has a drastic policy on population control. Yes, baby girls are most affected. Yes, it hurts to think what could have happened to her. Depending on the situation, our daughters' reactions and our reserves of tolerance, we answer, confirm and try to steer the talk away from painful words like "abandoned." At least while she's listening in.

I prefer to think that most people do not mean to offend and so I try to be informative, boasting about her accomplishments and waxing enthusiastic about Chinese culture. But then it comes, way too often, the stranger's cheery conclusion: "She's a lucky girl!"

I can't help but wince. Yes, she has a room full of toys and a college fund, a doting father and brother, a well-meaning if impatient mother. But please don't tell her she's lucky, that she should be grateful to have someone to raise her. That's surely the minimum that every child deserves. If you think I'm some selfless humanitarian, that I've done her a favor, you haven't heard me get on her case when it's forty-five minutes after her bedtime.

But is she lucky? I can't forget that she lost something irretrievable when her biological parents decided they would or could not raise her. She lost something else again when she was carted on board that flight out of Beijing. Maybe growing up adored will fill up her spaces and then the early trauma will shrink in importance. I hope. But I will not disrespect her personal history by pretending that being left parentless for eleven months was "lucky."

No, we're the lucky ducks, my husband and I, with our wish for a healthy girl miraculously granted in a hotel lobby in Hefei in October 2000.

Fortunate, too, are the other parents writing here, sharing their perspectives on an exceptional but joyful twist of fate. In this collection, the lucky ones write about their reasons for adopting from China, as well as the surprises, frustrations, and delights that have followed. Others explore the many dimensions of raising a child who is sometimes different from the crowd and sometimes just like any other kid.

The embracing of thousands of Chinese babies by North American and European families is a social experiment with no exact precedent, a demographic upheaval whose consequences aren't fully known. Yet.

No doubt many, maybe most, girls will grow up to enjoy happily ordinary lives. There may be others who never recover from being abandoned, deprived of their birthright, wounded by racial stereotypes, or adopted by inept — or worse — parents.

But this book captures where the experiment stands now, a

point at which we have reason to think that everything may work out just fine.

The evidence these essays offer is reassuring. Some stories here, Evan Solomon's or Denise Davy's, for example, may have begun amid terrible pain and loss. But our families are healing fast and prospering. Babies are growing up into confident, articulate young people, aware of who they are and where they're going. I think of Shelley's Page daughter Cleo, all of six years old, explaining *in Mandarin* to Chinese villagers: "We are Canadian, and I come from China." I think of teenagers Jasmine Bent and Lia Calderone, whose current goals include saving the world, seeing the Great Wall, and acing grade 11 math.

Or consider single father Douglas Hood, who wrote back in 1995 about his daughter Suki exploding into his life like a firecracker. Douglas's piece, with its irreverent approach to parenthood, made me laugh out loud when I read it years ago. I wondered about how it had gone and was delighted to be able track him down through the prodigious online network of adoptive parents. I was even more delighted when he agreed to write "Our Silk Road," an update of their lives together, now that Suki is sixteen. Never mind the teenage troubles; all signs are that Suki will make a splash.

Thinking about Doug's spirited if unorthodox parenting makes it all the more poignant to remember that China has tightened its rules on international adoption. Single parents no longer stand much chance of receiving a child. In May 2007, overwhelmed by the demand for children as the number available has dropped, Chinese officials instituted new policies, giving preference to married couples between 30 and 50. Would-be single parents are out of luck now, as is anyone with a chronic illness or disability, including obesity. The Chinese say they simply want the best chance of success and security for the children. That's surely what we've all wanted too. Yet, the good news that fewer children are being abandoned means bad news for those now unable to adopt from China.

We hope that our stories will convey what our children have lost, what we have found, and why we believe that we're the lucky ones.

Foreword
Jan Wong

WHEN I WAS A FOREIGN CORRESPONDENT in Beijing, "good news" stories were hard to find. I had been posted there in 1988. One year later, the Chinese government slaughtered hundreds, perhaps thousands, of unarmed protesters. Try as I might, for several years after that it was hard to write on any subject that was not somehow, directly or indirectly, connected to the Tiananmen Square massacre.

The one shining exception was the Chinese adoption story. It was a win-win situation, or to put it in Chinese terms, it was double happiness. Unwanted baby girls got a loving family and home. Foreign parents desperate for a child got one. And to put it bluntly, they got a healthy baby free of fetal alcohol syndrome, drug addiction, or any maternal ties.

The adoption story struck a chord with me. More than a century ago, a peasant in the Pearl River delta journeyed into Canton (now Guangzhou), the provincial capital. He carried two willow baskets balanced on a bamboo shoulder pole. It was circa 1886. China was still recovering from the aftermath of the Taiping Rebellion, which had devastated southern China and caused twenty million deaths.

That peasant was my great-grandfather. In the baskets were his two baby girls, my great-aunt and her sister, my maternal grandmother. My great-grandfather stood on the street corner and offered them to any passerby who would feed them. According to family history, my grandmother and great-aunt were adopted by a judicial official. He must have been enlightened because he gave them one year's education, enough so they could read and write.

Perhaps because he was enlightened, or perhaps because he didn't see the point of going to all that trouble for two unwanted babies, the official didn't bind the little girls' feet. In dynastic China, three-inch "lotus" feet were as coveted and erotic as cleavage is today in Hollywood. Having big, ugly feet greatly dimmed my grandmother's marriage prospects.

Meanwhile, my paternal grandfather had arrived in Canada in 1881. He was one of thousands of coolies recruited from the Pearl River delta to build the Canadian Pacific Railway. He was forty by the time he went back to China to look for a bride. It's my theory — based on nothing more than a professional habit of stringing together a bunch of unrelated facts into a coherent story — that all those years my grandfather spent in Canada, surrounded by beautiful Canadian women with their big feet, made him amenable to my grandmother's. Of course, it helped that she was sixteen and very pretty. But that's another story.

I stumbled upon the adoption story when I began noticing white people in Beijing with Chinese babies. I talked to the parents, and discovered they were almost all Canadians. A few quick calls to the Canadian embassy confirmed that the number of adopting parents was growing rapidly. Canada initially dominated the trend, apparently because a few pioneering Canadians had set up agencies specializing in Chinese adoptions.

I learned that one Beijing hotel, the Kunlun, received so many adoptive parents that they had hired a team of in-house babysit-ters, acquired dozens of cribs, and purchased a fleet of fold-up strollers. The Canadian embassy was so busy with the adoptions that it designated a person whose main job was handling the stressed-out parents. Red tape included health checks for the ba-bies and Canadian visas. The little girls, of course, all traveled to Canada on Chinese passports.

For the story in my newspaper, *The Globe and Mail*, I followed one couple from Montreal. Carrying their new Chinese infant daughter, they drew curious stares. At the Silk Market, I translated for a stall vendor who asked what they were doing with a Chinese baby. When he heard they were adopting her and taking her to Montreal, he grinned and said, "Adopt *me!*"

In an essay on dialectical materialism, Chairman Mao said that a bad thing can turn into its opposite. He was right. Chinese females are so unwanted, so unloved, that they are abandoned. They are left under bridges, in hospital waiting rooms, near police stations. If they survive, they end up in orphanages. And some of those despised little girls go on to a new life in the West where they are cherished, fed, clothed, and educated. They are given every chance to flourish, and more.

Many people read the story, and contacted me asking how they could adopt. At the time, the *Globe*'s foreign editor, my boss, was a young woman named Ann Rauhala. Ann went on to adopt a Chinese baby girl herself. She is also the creative force and the editor for this poignant book of first-person essays.

Each person in this book tells the same story, a love story. But each is unique. One parent is shocked — happily so — to discover she has been given a boy. Another fears her daughter might be discriminated against in her homogeneous Ontario town. Others talk about the developmental challenge facing an infant who has spent a year or more immobile in her crib. Still others worry about

3

the implications of uprooting their daughter from her language and culture. They wonder about the mothers who abandoned their daughters, pressured by China's one-child policy and influenced by an age-old cultural preference for sons. Meanwhile, the population sex imbalance in rural China is severe. In some villages, it has reached a ratio of 120 boys to 100 girls. That is not just because baby girls are abandoned; many are aborted on the basis of an ultrasound test, even though medical workers aren't supposed to tell parents the sex of the fetus.

The adoption story continues to evolve. At first, adoptive parents were allowed only one baby, the rule stemming somewhat absurdly from China's own one-child policy. I knew of one Canadian family who adopted one twin girl, then waited in agony for permission, granted months later, to adopt the marooned sister. Later it became possible to adopt more than one child. China even loosened restrictions on age and marital status. Single people could adopt. Gays could, too, although they could not be open about their sexuality because China only recently removed homosexuality from a list of psychiatric "disorders." More recently, China has imposed age limits. And it will no longer consider single parents.

The first Chinese adoptees are growing up. They're in their teens and early twenties, having bat mitzvahs, going to the mall, winning prizes at school. I see them in Chinese restaurants with their parents, each completely at home and comfortable in her skin.

During my stint as a foreign correspondent in Beijing from 1988 to 1994, I gave birth to two boys. I love my sons dearly, but I've always yearned for a daughter. When I was leaving for the airport in 1994, I had a last lunch with the Chinese woman who had been our nanny. She suddenly leaned across the dining room table and said to me, "Do you want to adopt a baby girl?"

Ben was then four and Sam was one. My husband felt we already couldn't cope. "No!" he shouted, at the same time as I shouted, "Yes!" It turned out that our nanny knew of a young woman, one of millions of migrants in Beijing whose menstrual cycle isn't being monitored by any government organization. She had just had her third child — her third *daughter*. Naturally, she and her husband didn't want the baby. If I wanted, I could have her right away. No red tape.

I thought of using Sam's passport to smuggle her out of China and into Canada. I figured that as a dual citizen (my husband, Norman, is American) my one-year-old could get back to Canada on his U.S. passport. But in the end, I lost my nerve. It is illegal, of course, to traffic in babies. Back in Canada, I often thought of her. I wondered if she had enough to eat, if anyone held her. I wondered if she was even alive. I never learned her name. In my mind, I called her the Ten-Minute Baby because if I had had enough nerve, I could have had a baby in ten minutes.

On a recent return trip to China, I asked our former nanny for news of the baby girl. She didn't know what had happened to her, didn't even know her name. She was puzzled that I seemed so fixated on the baby. "You can get a baby girl anywhere," she told me with a shrug. *"Duo de hen."* There are so many of them, she said.

As Traditional as a Child

Tess Kalinowski

OLIVIA IS WALKING INTO the dining room. She hangs on tightly to my dad's fingers. I know from experience his back must feel like it's breaking as he repeatedly indulges her desire to move.

My baby is grinning from ear to ear, her little head bobbing up and down, spontaneous giggles issuing from the pure pleasure of her own cleverness. Less than two months ago when I picked her up in China, she couldn't sit up for more than a few seconds without flopping onto her face.

Now on a perfectly ordinary Sunday for no reason other than that she is beautiful and healthy, intense joy is nudging tears to my eyes.

"I did that. I went and got us that," I say to my mother. Her arms are already outstretched to the grinning child stepping through the doorway.

Not being married seldom bothered me. Not having children was, for a long time, tearing me apart. To say my biological clock was ticking wouldn't be correct. I felt no physical imperative to give birth and my notions of children don't include the creation of a replica of myself or a partner.

I don't know whether other people genuinely have those feelings. I do know that the sound of time marching forward started to resonate when I was about thirty-three. By thirty-five, it was deafening.

It took me a long time to get past the embarrassment of wanting anything as traditional as a child.

I had a career that had exceeded my expectations. I had a house; smart, funny friends; and a devoted family. I understood how enviable my life was and I think that's why it became increasingly important to share it — not just the stuff, but the people and the laughter that just got better as I aged.

I'd spent a lifetime making alternative choices. Becoming a mother was practically the only thing I'd always been absolutely sure I wanted.

I had always enjoyed a wonderful relationship with my own mother. I wanted to continue that journey with another generation.

It takes me a moment to comprehend it's my daughter's Chinese name being called in the Hefei Holiday Inn meeting room. It's 9 a.m. Monday. My sister and I are among ten adoptive Canadian families who flew from Vancouver to Beijing on Saturday and then flew two hours southeast to Hefei on Sunday.

Finally we are gathered in the room where babies from the nearby city of Chuzou are already waiting with their caregivers.

The other members of the group I've been assigned by the Ottawa-based Children's Bridge agency, have, by process of elimination, figured out that the floppy baby with the Elvis sideburns is mine. It is February 28. The pictures I received at Christmas were taken in October. I have trouble seeing the resemblance. Nevertheless, I'm moved to tears at the sight of my daughter.

A young woman brings Fu Yuan Qin, who I'll call Olivia, toward me. I squeak a first hello but don't immediately take her in my arms. I've gone to the adoption seminars and know enough to introduce my voice and touch slowly.

Once Olivia is in my arms the nanny retreats across the room. Later I will persuade her to hold Olivia for a photograph.

Olivia has a cold. Her cheeks are flaming from teething and the odor of urine-soaked wool is rising from her damp little body. The humid meeting room is easily twenty-three degrees Celsius. In the Chinese custom, Olivia is wearing several layers of clothing.

My sister Katherine holds the miserable infant for three hours while I complete the adoption paperwork. As instructed by our guide and interpreter, Ding, I repeatedly write my promise to always care for the child and never abandon her.

Ding will later translate so the adoptive parents can ask the orphanage director about our babies' lives to that point. He stresses we are not to ask any questions about the girls' birth parents or where the child was abandoned.

I can see from across the room that Olivia is crying and, despite disapproving looks from the Chinese, Katherine has stripped the baby down to a fresh diaper and top. Without the pants, we can see Olivia won't straighten one leg. It is tucked tightly next to her little body. I'm worried enough to mention this to another adoptive parent, a pediatric nurse. He promises to stop by later and have a look.

Before we are released from the room, the adoptive parents are interviewed by a notary. Ding translates her questions.

Photo by Catherine Farquharson

Am I sure I want to take this baby girl back to Canada?

I know my baby looks miserable and ill. Of the ten babies being adopted that day, mine is looking among the least healthy. In the split-second before I answer, it occurs to me the notary is offering to have a different baby brought for me.

I smile and insist, "Oh yes, this is the baby girl I want to take home."

Adopting a child is invasive and exhausting. There's a rigid bureaucratic process but the experience is unique to each family.

It took me eighteen months of research, rigorous paperwork, and rushing for appointments before I finally found myself flying to China.

Anyone with the right biology can make a child, but adoption in Ontario requires a Ministry of Community and Social Services home-study approval. To get it, you undergo intense scrutiny. You pay a social worker to interview you, to review your home, your job, your finances, and your relationships. You must get friends, family, and colleagues to write reference letters.

There are virtually no healthy infants available for public adoption in Ontario. Today, fewer women put their babies up for adoption than before and those who do frequently opt for private adoption so they can select the baby's parents. Public adoptions are limited mostly to special needs and older children but it's a hard truth that most people want healthy infants.

Eastern Europe and China are the most established avenues for Canadians seeking overseas adoptions.

Because China's single-child policy allows only one child per family, that country has thousands of unwanted babies, almost all girls. Kept in state-run orphanages, the girls who aren't adopted will be schooled and supported until they are eighteen. The orphanages also house some boys and special-needs children.

Although I didn't visit Olivia's orphanage in Chuzhou, our group was permitted to tour a facility in Hefei where some of the other children had been kept. Those babies were healthier and better developed than the Chuzhou babies in our group. The director of the Hefei orphanage told us there are about 400 children in its care. About 200 of those live in foster homes.

Most children adopted from China are developmentally delayed as a result of their extended institutionalization. In Hefei there were only two or three staff looking after dozens of infants. There were toys in the children's playroom but they were mostly on shelves in boxes.

Most of our group wept at the sight of so many children milling about like ducks in a pen. One little boy, about two, with no arms below the elbow, was riding a plastic toy while another child tried to push him. Another little girl ran wildly among the Canadians pulling on us and smiling in a desperate bid for attention.

The director told us that only about thirty-five percent of the Hefei children would be adopted — only fifteen percent internationally.

Typically, the adopted children catch up within a few months of arriving in their new homes where they receive stimulation and love. When I got Olivia, she was eleven months old and couldn't sit up. It was less than a month before she was sitting up straight, and a few weeks later she was trying to walk.

A Chinese adoption typically costs between $15,000 and $20,000 Canadian, including a two-week trip for two to China. Children's Bridge arranges a week in the child's home province in which a birth certificate and certificate of abandonment are notarized and the child's Chinese passport is prepared. The second week is spent in Beijing, where the child undergoes a medical exam necessary for an entry visa into Canada, the only Western country that requires this medical.

I talked to a woman who adopted from Russia. She had taken a second mortgage on her home. Many families max out credit cards and lines of credit. The National Bank of Canada offers a special adoption loan program.

Early in my research one woman put it this way: Adoption is the price of a car. It may be a compact model or it may be a luxury sedan, but it's just a car.

It's common for adopting couples to have endured the trauma of fertility treatment. The first adoption seminar I attended at the Adoption Council of Ontario in Toronto included half a dozen couples and myself. The common element in that room was grief. Young women recounted multiple miscarriages and unsuccessful hormone treatments. Their partners sat beside them, stoic and helpless.

When adoption was still a possibility for single people, I was among the growing number of single women choosing to adopt. It was rare and difficult for an unmarried man to adopt, but, in the course of my research, I heard of one man who obtained a child from Russia.

When I adopted Olivia, China had no trouble with single women adopting. There were three single mothers in our group of ten families. I often consider that a generation or two back, motherhood wasn't an option for most unmarried women.

Back in our hotel room, we give Olivia a sponge bath and a bottle.

The pediatric nurse stops in and finds one of her legs a little weaker than the other but doesn't think there's anything to worry about. He checks her with a stethoscope and assures us the cold hasn't moved into her chest.

About midnight Olivia's crying wakes us. But it's a different baby who gets out of the crib. After a bottle and clean diaper she is more than content but not tired. It's the middle of the night. I'm as far from home as I ever expect to be and this small stranger has decided she'd like to play. Between the hours of midnight and 2 a.m., I catch my first glimpse of the daughter I'll be carrying back to Canada. She chuckles and coos, wants to be thrown in the air and caught, tickled and bounced on the bed. I'm exhausted but relieved beyond words.

Sometime after 2 a.m., Olivia goes back to sleep for about three hours. At 5 a.m. she's up again entertaining Katherine and me. We know it's late at home but we call our parents to tell them we've got our baby and she's going to be just fine. A world away, we can feel their urgency to hold their first grandchild.

Tumbling Down

Patricia Hluchy

TWO WEEKS BEFORE I BECAME a mother, my house fell down.
It was a Saturday morning, 3 o'clock, mid-January, the darkest
depths of winter, and then the sound of an avalanche — bricks
were falling off the front of our house as the roof crumpled and
the front wall broke away, leaning out about fifteen degrees. I had a
monster head cold and wanted to pretend nothing was happening.
However, my husband, Hamish, jumped out of bed and rushed to
the front bedroom. He came back telling me to get up, get dressed,
and get the hell out, lest the whole structure collapse on us.

This is what had happened. In January 1999, Toronto experienced unprecedented snowfall. By January 13, the amount of snow
was already double the average for the month, and it had arrived in
a series of nasty blizzards. Mayor Mel Lastman called in the army
to help plow and, one imagines, to keep the citizenry from rioting
over the outrageously vile weather. We live at the end of a row of

twelve houses, and that night the roof of the dwelling six doors north fell in because of its burden of snow. That caused a domino effect down the row. Our house sustained the least damage, but it still took more than four months to fix.

After we'd pushed against three feet of snow outside our door, I rushed back in to get a sedative, prescribed so I could sleep on the plane to China. I figured our insurance wouldn't cover this disaster and that my dream come true, one-year-old Wu Zhi, who was living in an orphanage in Hubei province, was no longer within reach. There was no way I'd sleep without medication. After standing around among firefighters and police, at 4:30 a.m. we trudged four blocks to my sister's house, where I did manage to sleep a little.

Fortunately, our insurance covered the devastation. Hamish and I spent the next two weeks camped out at my sister's. The sympathetic managing editor at *Maclean's* magazine, where I was entertainment editor, told me I could take paid leave to deal with the calamity and to get ready for China. About a week after the collapse, we spent a few hours outside our wreck of a house in the biting cold as workmen brought out all our possessions, destined for storage. We went through every box, every hastily filled garbage bag, to extract what we'd need during our two-week China sojourn and afterward — our collection of baby bottles and clothes, toys, our own clothing, and other personal items. Inevitably, things went missing, including the tray of the highchair. (We spent the first several weeks with our baby daughter without that essential platform — anyone who's fed a one-year-old knows just how chaotic that would be.)

Difficult as it was, the travel to China and our two weeks there were a relief — an escape from the stress and aggravation of dealing with the insurance adjuster, two contractors (one working on the exterior and one inside) and various workmen. And there was the exquisite joy of meeting our daughter and discovering her to be alert and healthy, not to mention in possession of great charm. Zhi screamed for five hours that first day, in two bouts of equal duration. We knew this was a good sign: clearly, she was attached to the caregivers at the orphanage, which meant she was more likely to bond with us. Even amid the howling and her repeated pointing at the door — "Get me out of here!" — I fell in love with her.

Adoption is a dauntingly abrupt transition from childlessness to parenthood; there's no nine-month gestation to allow you to get used to the idea. And because Zhi was already thirteen months old and overdue for wandering about and exploring her surroundings, we had to hit the ground running.

With the house disaster, it felt as if we'd been violently wrenched out of our old existence, and then had to rebuild our lives, and our home.

I learned when I was nineteen that I could not have children because of a medical condition. I had undergone tests in a Victoria hospital, and the gynecologist came in on the second day to brusquely tell me my equipment was flawed. My dreams, my sense of self, came tumbling down. No babies of my own. I ran to a pay phone to call my mother, who lived an hour's drive away.

It was pretty much the end of my youth. My childhood hadn't been particularly blissful, but until that day my hopes were essentially intact. I would not fully recover from the blow for another twenty-six years, until February 2, 1999, the day Zhi came into my life.

I was one of those girls who'd always thought of herself as a mother-in-training. It was like the call to nunhood that I half expected as a devout and tortured Catholic in my childhood and early teens. That call never arrived, but by the age of nine or ten

I knew that in order to be fully me I had to be a mum one day. Coming of age with feminism — I was born in 1952 — meant that I also expected to break away from the generations of hard-working but uneducated and domestically anchored mothers who came before me on my father's Slovak side and in my mother's Italian clan. My parents did not expect any more of me — they even tried to dissuade me from going to university despite my strong marks in school. Nevertheless, I expected to have an interesting job one day, and mostly I thought of teaching (some maternal impulse was no doubt part of that), though journalism was a dare-not-hope-for-it dream. Above all else, marriage and motherhood would be the clinchers of my life.

The news of my infertility changed everything. It unleashed a tendency to melancholy that was already there. There's probably some irony in the fact that, feeling my womanhood was compromised, I reacted in a way that is, in our culture, quintessentially feminine: I directed my anger and disappointment inside, where they could morph into depression.

"Barren" has to be the most brutal, most hopeless word in the English language. And hopeless I became. In my second year of university I took a philosophy course on existentialism. This may be self-flattery, but I seem to recall I was one of the few students who kind of got Sartre's *Being and Nothingness*. It resonated for me, viscerally.

For years, I felt like an outsider — a bitter one — among other women. If someone commented on my "breeder" hips, I might smolder for hours. It was difficult to weather the pregnancies of a few friends who conceived in their twenties, right after university. Sadness also turned to self-destruction. I drank — or at least *tried* to drink — like the guys. I did reckless things and gravitated toward reckless lovers. I tried to fashion a tough-chick persona, but mostly people found my attempts comical: who was

Photo by Catherine Farquharson

this pallid, wimpy-looking, sentimental girl with a penchant for floral, feminine clothing (that I just couldn't shed) who used the word "fuck" ridiculously often? It wasn't just knowledge of my inability to have children that darkened my youth. There were other factors, of course, in my constitution and in my past. But infertility became the focal point of my despair.

Through it all, I continued to adore babies and older kids. And I did think about adoption, even as I narcissistically mourned the little boy or girl who would have looked like me and inherited only my good qualities. In retrospect, I feel lucky in comparison to women who learn of their infertility, and/or that of their partner, when they're thirty or forty. I had all those years to accommodate myself to — to become excited by — the prospect of raising a kid with whom I'd have no biological connection. I read books and articles about adoption. I'd cry over photos of heretofore sorrowful women with their South Asian or Caucasian or Native daughter or son. As I thought of my own family and those of my friends, I realized that biology does not necessarily make for understanding or love or harmony between parent and child.

And though I'd always been an avid and loving babysitter, I learned at twenty-one that I really could love other people's children. For four months in 1972, I was an au pair in Paris, looking after Emmanuelle and François Skyvington, ages seven and four. I adored them. There was some ego in my zealous guardianship, but I was surprised at how much I relished their delight and happiness. I knew — I really knew — that I had to be an adoptive mom, and that I'd be a loving one.

The prospect of transracial adoption was never a problem. Besides, I was a pragmatist. My friends were all using birth control or, on rare occasion, terminating pregnancy. I knew that the supply of domestic children for adoption was drying up. And transracial adoption appealed to my idealism. Color-blind love seemed something the world needed.

In my mid-thirties I finally married someone who seemed a good match and who said he wanted to adopt. But that relationship failed. Finally, I met Hamish, and after a few years we were ready to become parents.

By then, I was forty-five. Some friends and family told me I was too old, that I should close that door, even though they knew how ardently I'd wanted to be a mother. I'm glad I stuck to my guns. I was right about how much I would cherish parenthood even though I hadn't yet realized how much it can enrich one's life, how it can make you feel more fully human, more linked to the community, a real part of the life of this planet. Nor did I anticipate how looking after a child can expand and uplift you. Loving my daughter has been the closest thing I've experienced to transcendence in this life. Sure, we squabble at times, I yell at her some mornings, and there are days when I think I'm a lousy mother.

But here's the thing: I always assumed in an unthinking way that parenthood would be about me and my needs, about personal redemption. Childrearing, of course, turns out not to be like that at all. It's about the kid, or the kids, and all the vitality and promise they hold. It's a love that expects little in return, and sometimes gets little or nothing back. It's a pure affirmation of life, the best thing that ever happened to me.

We still live in the infamous house, its roof now buttressed every which way. While the repairs were being made, we took the opportunity to renovate the kitchen and knock down walls to create, yes, a family room. When we moved back in with Zhi one warm weekend in May, it felt like a new place, fresh and bright. Full of possibility.

Double Happiness

Evan Solomon

THERE ARE TWO FIRSTS.

In China, it arrives as a flood. Our daughter is carried through the doors of the waiting room inside the Guangdong adoption center, eight months old and barely thirteen-and-a-half pounds. She's placed in my arms and I bring her close. My breath is sob-soaked and gasping. Video cameras whirl and whirl so nothing, not the first second, the first embrace, the first kiss, will be ever be forgotten. Curious, our daughter reaches out to touch my face. I smile as if all is somehow instantly perfect. But then something changes. What? She's crying. Crying hard. My wife, Tammy, takes her into a tight embrace and rocks her back and forth. In a room now drenched in tears, we soothe. Touch. Whisper. The small works of love. After so much planning, so many social workers, fingerprints, documents, passports, so much waiting and waiting, staring at the first mystical photograph of this little girl, and waiting even more, after all this scaffolding built to support this one moment, we are here at last trying hard not to get washed away by the flood of it all. Maizie Elizabeth Ai Nuan. Our daughter. A family.

Like any birth — and yes, this is a special kind of birth — our adoption day is part miracle, replete with wonder and mystery. Wonder at how this perfect little girl came to us, wonder at her ability to adapt, at her smile and how her face softens into sleep. Wonder at how, within hours of taking her back to our hotel, she is in the bath and elated. Water. She loves it. Coos. Splashes. I am so overjoyed at her happiness that impulse takes over. Let's take her for a swim in the hotel pool. "The pool? Now?" The other parents think we've gone mad. "You can't do that stuff yet." We bundle up in bathing suits and towels and walk through the lobby, carrying our daughter. Some hard looks. *You people are not ready to parent.* But in the water Maizie's tears turn to laughter, a pattern that will become her signature. We float on wonder, how we three — Tammy, Maizie, and I — have become a universe of one.

Beneath the wonder, though, something else: a series of subterranean catacombs housing the mysteries of Maizie's past. What is her medical history and what might she grow up to look like? Who are Maizie's birth parents and what are their circumstances? As we swim in the pool, ecstatic, what are they doing? There are no points of reference, no solid information. Just a sense that, for every moment of togetherness we have, there might be someone's countermoment of separateness, another life connected to our daughter, complete with a biological mother and father just like us. We cannot ever know this other story, but somehow we want to honor it. It is part of our beginning. The existential questions raised by China's closed adoption process are so daunting because there is so little that we North Americans can do about it. There is no blame. It is what it is, a hard choice made in China in 1979 by a government facing a hard situation: an exploding population promising mass poverty that might be alleviated by a necessary if draconian one-child policy. Still, as parents, we want to give our daughter any answers that she might want. Information is power, and even now, as we fuse as a family, we feel powerless. And parents do not do powerless well.

Still, I'm used to the feeling. Building a family has been a long lesson in powerlessness. I always assumed it would be a simple matter. Love. Marriage. Children. That the logic of these steps is such a cliché only deepened my sense of entitlement. If it's a cliché I guess anyone can have it. And adoption was always part of the plan. I had lived in China where I worked as a reporter for a year in the early 1990s, and when I returned home I promised that when I got married I would adopt from China. I met Tammy years later and she, too, always wanted to adopt. In the happy arrogance of love, we fully expected our plan to work. Four kids: two biological, two adopted from China. Perfect. We got busy.

Just months after our wedding, we got in touch with the Open Arms Agency, contacted a social worker, and began the adoption process. We wanted our future adopted children to know that they were as much a priority as our biological ones. But while the adoption process was slow and bogged down with paperwork, our pregnancy process was even slower. Slow as in not happening.

Months passed. Then a year. We could not get pregnant and, in a horrible bit of mimicry, our adoption process also ground to a halt. SARS hit and everything from China shut down. I got a bit paranoid, I'll admit it. Was something actively trying to prevent us from having a child? By then Tammy and I were deep into the maze of fertility treatments. They tested us for everything and found nothing. As in the case of twenty-five percent of infertile couples, there was simply no explanation for our situation. Powerless. In response, we deployed every medical and pseudo-medical weapon available. We ate special foods. Gave up every possible vice, even hot showers. We tried inseminations. IVFS. Nothing.

They say that after death and divorce, infertility is the most traumatic thing a couple can go through. Maybe. I can tell you it is hard on both sides, but the truth is, the woman bears the brunt of it. While I had to deal with the standard male jibes —"Hey, how come no kids yet? You don't know how to load your gun?"— and give the odd sperm sample (a job, let's face it, most men really don't mind), my wife went through something else entirely. Hundreds of examinations. Mystical-sounding medicines of every kind, one actually extracted from the urine of Italian nuns. (What those poor pissing nuns had to go through I shall never know!) And the needles. My wife became a pincushion. Infertility is, like so many medical conditions, another land entirely, a pitiless place that you survive through gallows humor, patience, and, if you are me, being married to some kind of hero.

After trying everything, after the hope and, in this privatized part of our medical system, after the money spent . . . failure. To tweak a line from Farley Mowat, we were lost in the barrens, literally. Barren. My pathetic little family plan withered away.

And just then, the SARS crisis ended. Shortly after, our adoption papers came through. Rescue. As my memory now selectively relates, it's as if one-two-three, we are in China and nothing else matters but Maizie. The flood washes the past away. Of course, it is not really like that. Adoption does not really wash away the pain of infertility. The two are different. But then, infertility does not in any way diminish the joy of adoption. A child is a miracle, any way he or she arrives, and it is not about what she does to your past, it is about how she transforms your future.

We arrive home triumphantly. Exhausted from jet lag, sleep deprivation, and new parenting, we decide to throw a party to celebrate New Year's Eve with our first child. Our friends arrive. Corks pop. We let it all out.

Three weeks later, our second first.

It is a cloudless January day. The cold bites clean. Tammy calls me from her mobile phone, sounding fraught.

"Are you busy?" she asks.

"What's the matter? Is Maizie okay?"

"She's fine. We're sitting in the car, outside your office. Can you come down for a sec?"

I rush down to the car and see that Maizie has fallen asleep in her car seat. She wears a cream-colored hat and scarf that Tammy has knit for her, the same one she wore on another cold day, outside of Beijing, when we all walked a section of the Great Wall. I get in the front and Tam immediately pulls out a white plastic stick.

"What's this?"

She pauses.

"A pregnancy test. Look at the line. Positive."

I don't react until we whip up to the drug store to get another. After all, these things are only, like, 99.99 percent accurate. I had to be sure. Another blue line.

Nine months later — and now I am entitled to my family cliché — our son Gideon is born. A second miracle. How did this happen with no medical intervention? We don't know, and frankly, in our gratitude, we don't bother to investigate. But around us explanations abound. We are told countless times that our so-called miracle is actually a common occurrence. "Oh, yes, this always happens," someone says knowingly. "Often people are too stressed to get pregnant, then they adopt a baby and relax and they get pregnant." Voila! Mystery solved. As if infertility is just a matter of stress. Our fault actually. Why couldn't we just relax? As if women do not get pregnant during war. And as if adoption is not, in and of itself, a valid endeavor. Its true power must be as a medicinal cure for infertile couples. I know this sounds bitter, and yes, the people who explain all this mean well. They simply do not know the experience. But still, it is a persistent myth and it is wrong. It is not, in fact, a common phenomenon, though if it were, all the better. The people who understand this best are the other families with whom we went to China to adopt our girls. We talk to them openly about it and they talk to us about their own unique challenges or journeys. They understand that not all mysteries have an easy answer.

As with Maizie, we survive the flood of Gideon's arrival on a raft of wonder. At the hospital, happy chaos. Maizie's godmother pulls me aside and says, "You've had two firsts now. Adoption and biological. Double happiness."

It's a uniquely Chinese idea. The character for double happiness is a symbol for good luck. Brides and grooms often adorn their weddings with it, hoping their future life will be blessed. The origins of the symbol come from a Tang Dynasty folk tale. A young man on his way to the capital to take his final exams suddenly falls ill. Rescued by a village herbalist and his daughter, he is nursed back to health in time to make his exams. But he doesn't want to leave. He's fallen in love with the daughter. She agrees to marry him if, after finishing his exams, he returns to her and completes the verses to a half-finished poem she recites. He takes his leave. In the capital the young man comes first in the exams and is brought before the emperor. To see just how wise the young man really is, the emperor recites a half-completed poem and challenges the student to complete it. The young man realizes that the perfect answer to the emperor's poem is the verse the herbalist's daughter has told him back in the village. When he recites her verse, the emperor is delighted and rewards him greatly. The young man marries the girl. One stretch of bad luck has turned into two pieces of good luck. Double happiness.

A few weeks after our own kind of double happiness, one of the parents we met in China takes me aside. "Was it different?" he asks. "The feeling you had in China when you got Maizie and in the hospital when you got Gideon?" It is a question of difference and I am asked it again and again. Does blood trump love? I do not even hesitate in my answer. "No," I say. "Not at all. There is not a molecule of difference between the two feelings. It was and is just joy. Love." He smiles, as if relieved. I am not trying to comfort him with my answer, just telling him the truth. It is like when someone looks at you with your Chinese daughter and says, "Did you adopt her from an orphanage? Oh, she's very lucky." But we adopted parents all know that we are the real lucky ones, not the girls. We're both lucky. Double happiness.

Our two children have different backgrounds. We often talk about their individual birth stories. We respect their uniqueness and we know that, as time passes, each will struggle with their own identity issues. That's what growing up is all about — making sense of things, orienting yourself in the wider world. For us, double happiness is not just a gift. It is a challenge. A covenant. To raise a family as one while honoring the ones in the family. That is our singular kind of happiness.

At Lingyin Si

Susan Olding

AT LINGYIN SI, a temple in the city of Hangzhou, women come to pray for fertility. Although the name, translated variously as "Palace of the Hidden Immortals," "Temple of Inner Seclusion," and "Temple of the Soul's Retreat," suggests an oasis of tranquility and calm, the place is wildly popular with Chinese and Westerners alike, and all day long its crimson halls echo with the snap, gaggle, and stomp of tourists. Zen monks remain in residence, but the clink of cash registers rings louder than the chime of prayer bells.

That does not deter the hopeful. On a hot September morning, I stood inside the temple gates with a friend and our newly adopted infant daughters. Together we watched as one young woman paid her respects to Guan Yin, Goddess of Mercy. Dropping coins into a wrought-iron urn, she gathered sticks of incense and laid them, smoking, at the altar. There, they lay against a hill of fruit, flowers, and two- and ten-yuan notes deposited by other suppli-cants. The girl's spiky haircut, fashionable clothes, and vivid makeup announced a modern sensibility, but the look on her face expressed reverence and fervent desire. Ignoring the pushing crowds, ignoring our prying eyes, she bowed and whispered her prayers.

Sensing a presence at my elbow, I turned. An elegantly dressed woman in her fifties, a stranger, leaned over the rim of the baby sling.

"Girl," she said, gesturing to the sleeping child.

I nodded.

"You have to go through long process. In your country also."

"Yes."

"How much you pay the Chinese government?"

My friend and I exchanged glances. Adoptive parents do not relish the imputation of baby-buying. I fussed with the carrier's straps, pulling my daughter closer and turning her face away from the stranger's. "A donation. To the orphanage," I said. "I put it in the director's hands."

"Ah. The *orphanage*." Sensing my coolness, the woman drew back. For a few minutes we spoke of other things — the heat, the pressing crowds. She asked my friend and me where we were from, and told us that she came from Macao. "Pretty girls. Lucky girls," she remarked before continuing on her way. "Lucky parents," we corrected.

Another tour group entered the temple enclosure, their voices raised in animated talk, their color-coded baseball caps bobbing. The young woman at the altar stood up as if to leave, but instead she went back to the iron urn, returning with another stick of incense.

"That was a strange question," said my friend.

I shrugged. "People have so many misconceptions."

At the age of one week, my daughter was delivered by local police to the Hangzhou Children's Welfare Institute. Located on the outskirts of the city near the site of an ancient, unexcavated tomb and surrounded by rice fields and orchards, the orphanage was largely rebuilt in 1994 after an earthquake. It stands on an enormous lot, and includes eight large buildings and several smaller ones. With its pristine clinic, its brightly tiled turrets, and its playgrounds, fountains, and stone pandas nestled amid the poplars, the complex looks like a peculiar hybrid of hospital and fantasy theme park. This is where my daughter spent her first ten months of life. I can only guess at the details; the Hangzhou Institute's "Brief History of Infants" is fewer than a hundred words long. But from that document and my own short visit, I know this much: That the cool light reflecting off the chrome cribs and the blue tile walls is the light she traced round the room. *Eye can follow the moving object to 180 degrees.* That here, from young women dressed in pink-and-white lab coats, she learned what it is to be cradled in someone's arms. *Shy, quiet, like to cuddle.* Here she tasted formula and juice. *Feed every three hours; feed when needed, no fix time.* Here she began the complicated tasks of motor and cognitive development. *When adult call her name, she can lift her head and look at the person.* Here, day after day, night after night, the coos and cries of other babies soothed and startled her.

Although they are not our children we take the responsibility of their parents, reads an orphanage brochure. To how many does the staff owe this responsibility? Before the earthquake, the institute held 150 beds; more were added during the renovations. State orphanages like the Hangzhou Institute exist in every major city in China; altogether there are seventy-three of them, housing as many as 20,000 children. In addition, smaller, privately run facilities and social welfare homes are common throughout the country. Reliable statistics about the total number of orphans at any given moment are difficult to obtain, but estimates have ranged anywhere between 17,000 and one million. A conservative figure, based on government sources, is 120,000 — the majority of them casualties of restrictive family planning laws, otherwise known as the "one-child policy." Most of these children will never be adopted.

The Chinese have a saying: Above are the halls of heaven; on earth, Suzhou and Hangzhou.

Achieving prominence as the southern end of the Grand Canal during the Sui dynasty between 581 and 618 AD, Hangzhou was also the capital of the Wuyue state, and the seat of the southern Song dynasty in the twelfth and thirteenth centuries. During this period, despite the bureaucratic factionalism of the Song court, China experienced unprecedented advances in agricultural technology and productivity, in commercialization and urbanization, in scholarship, literature, and all the arts. As the capital, Hangzhou was the hub of all this teeming activity. Shortly after its prime, the Venetian merchant Marco Polo claimed to have visited the place, calling it

> *The noble and magnificent Kin-sai, a name that signifies "The Celestial City," and which it merits from its pre-eminence to all others in the world, in point of grandeur and beauty, as well as from its abundant delights, which might lead an inhabitant to imagine himself in paradise.*[1]

A hundred miles in circuit, the city was crosshatched by hundreds of paved roads. Twelve thousand bridges spanned its numerous canals. Ten market squares and innumerable shops sold every conceivable good: the textiles and ceramics for which

---

[1] All quotations from Marco Polo are taken from Manuel Komroff's revision of the Marsden translation of *The Travels of Marco Polo (The Venetian)*. Liveright, 1926, 1933, 1982.

China is justly famous, but also wood, pearls, and handicrafts from Japan; ginseng and other medicinal herbs from Korea; spices, ivory, and jewels from India and the Middle East; and even silver from Mexico and Peru. By the late thirteenth century, the wealthy population numbered nearly two million. Courtesans practiced their seductive arts in every quarter. Theaters, many with multiple balconies, played to packed houses in seventeen separate amusement districts. Residents spent vast sums on their houses, furnishing them with floors inlaid with precious metals, ceilings adorned with elaborate carving, and opulent brocade tapestries. People wore silk; pets were dyed pink with balsam leaves. And day and night, carriages traversed the avenues, while dozens of beautifully painted pleasure barges cruised the famed West Lake.

> *The management of arms is unknown to them, nor do they keep any in their houses. They conduct their mercantile and manufacturing concerns with perfect candor and honesty. They are friendly toward each other, and persons who inhabit the same street, both men and women, from the mere circumstance of neighborhood, appear like one family.*

At each stage of our adoption, Chinese officials bestowed a gift on our daughter. A silk scarf. A stuffed bear. A piece of jade. A chop — a carved seal engraved with her name. To my husband and me, they gave documents. Passport. Birth certificate. Adoption certificate. And another certificate, unnamed. *Our institute has searched for her parents and relatives by all means, but no trace can be found.*

No trace.
A partial fiction, spelled out to appease the Gods of Bureaucracy.

It is the custom of the people of [Hangzhou], upon the birth of a child, for the parents to make a note, immediately, of the day, hour, and minute at which the delivery took place.

So wrote Marco Polo almost seven hundred years ago.

Undressing my daughter for admission, orphanage workers discovered a piece of paper. On it, her birth date appears in simple, even crude-looking characters. Nothing more.

The existence of a note implies a literate parent, but the rough calligraphy suggests someone without much education — or without much time. Whatever her circumstances, this someone troubled herself to find or beg or borrow or buy a pen and a piece of paper. She folded the paper into a tiny square, buried that square within the folds of the squirming baby's clothing, searched for a place to set the child — and walked away.

Why China, some people asked us when they heard of our plans to adopt. Oh, *China*, said others. Of *course*. They throw their girls away there, don't they?

Lingyin Si was founded in 326 AD. At one time, it consisted of nine towers, eighteen pavilions, seventy-five halls — a total of 300 rooms — and provided home to 3,000 monks. But in every century, war and other disasters have taken their toll; throughout its long history, the temple has been destroyed and rebuilt at least sixteen times. Most recently, only the intervention of Zhou Enlai saved it from complete devastation at the hands of Mao's Red Guards.

As with Lingyin Si, so with the city where it stands. Europeans sneered at Marco Polo's account of Hangzhou as being too fantastic to be believed — yet later travellers confirmed it. For many years, even after the invasion of the Mongol emperors who were Polo's employers, the city maintained its prominence and allure. Gradually, though, its harbor silted over, and trade moved first to Ningpo and later to Shanghai. The fine canals and roadways fell into disuse and disrepair, the market stalls stood empty. Calamity struck in 1861–1863, when Hangzhou was occupied by Taiping rebels, then recaptured by the Imperial army. In the ensuing fracas, the city was almost entirely destroyed and the bulk of its population was dispersed or killed.

The men as well as the women have fair complexions, and are handsome . . .

My daughter's complexion is fair and bright. Her cheeks flush pink with excitement, cool air, or anger. Her hair is fine and fast growing, her features delicate and regular, her lips the kind that people sometimes call bee-stung. From someone, she inherited these gifts, and more — her responsiveness to music, her strength and superior balance, her talent for mimicry, her delight in words. Inherited, too, is her temperament: not *shy, quiet,* as promised by the orphanage report, but active, expressive, spirited, intense. Content, she hums and babbles. Happy, she laughs, and her laugh strikes the air like a silver bell; there is nothing she likes better than to dance. Angry, she wails and thrashes. Only when frightened is she still.

Contemporary Hangzhou has regained much of its ancient luster. Arriving by air from Beijing, my husband, Mark, and I saw first a green and luxuriant landscape. Then came houses, hundreds and hundreds of them, each more than four storeys high, many of them bulging with balconies and capped with gleaming towers. Their tile roofs glistened in the sun like the scales of a million fishes. Apartment buildings, I assumed from their size, but the Chinese-born coordinator of our adoption agency assured me they were private family homes. "The tea," she said, gesturing back toward the rolling hills. "Farmers here are rich."

The city remains remarkable among urban centers in China for its green spaces and its human scale. The boardwalk surrounding West Lake and temples such as the Six Harmonies Pagoda and Lingyin Si do much to preserve the city's tranquil atmosphere. Yet these historic charms are threatened by the pace of development. In Hangzhou's moist air, the sounds of ten centuries or more co-mingle — the slap of water against the hull of a barge, the whisper of tea leaves tossed in a bamboo basket, but also the clatter of mechanical looms, the crash of wrecking balls, the buzz of pneumatic drills. One morning, as Mark and I left our hotel, we noticed workers beginning to lay the first bricks in a long wall. By sundown, the wall, a block in length and more than ten feet high, had been completed.

If you want to forsake a child, there are many places to do it. An alley, or a field, or a ditch will do. The end of a long road. In the midst of thick tea bushes.

My daughter was discovered at the entrance to People's Hospital Number Seven. Hospitals are notoriously busy places. People come and go at every hour, many of them employed by the government. As in most other countries, in China it is against the law to abandon a child. The penalties for being caught include fines of up to 5,000 yuan — more than half the annual income of an average worker in Hangzhou — and forced sterilization. If you want to abandon your child, a hospital is a risky place to do it.

On the other hand, many of the comers and goers to a hospital are doctors and nurses — people whose job it is to ensure the preservation of health, people who have pledged their own lives to protecting the lives of others. A hospital *is* a risky place to leave a child. Risky for the mother.

*To strangers also, who visit their city, they give proofs of
cordiality . . .*

City dwellers in China are now used to the sight of foreigners,
so in Hangzhou, we did not encounter the surprised stares that
would have met travellers from the West a decade or more ago.
Instead, we were greeted with smiles and attempts to communicate. Somehow, between our pathetically few words of Mandarin
and their schoolbook English, we managed. One afternoon, my
husband wandered alone into a busy restaurant. Unable to read
the menu, he tried as discreetly as possible to look at people's
plates in the hope of finding something to his taste that he could
point to. A young man sitting at a window table noticed him.
"Would you like something to eat?" he asked, in English. He
then described the offerings in some detail and invited Mark to
share a plate of tea-smoked duck, one of the specialties of the
house.

The sight of children evokes from the Chinese an even friend-
lier response. Evenings, on the West Lake boardwalk and on city
streets, we watched as parents by the hundreds slowed their pace
to match their toddlers'. Looking up, they met us with expectant
smiles. *Isn't he wonderful*, their faces said. Clearly, they were used
to seeing their delight mirrored in the eyes of others. After our
adoption, we became the focus of the same kind of attention.
"Chinese baby," people sometimes said. With those who could not
understand English, we often flashed a printed card explaining
in Chinese that she was ours by adoption. And everywhere, in
government offices, in parks, in restaurants, on busy streets, our
daughter's face and our laminated card were passports to wide,
enthusiastic grins, to renewed attempts at conversation, and to
that universal sign of approval, the thumbs up.

My daughter's birth mother kept her for one week. When she set the baby down, her body must have still ached from the delivery. Yet already she knew the child was healthy and strong. *Cries loudly, has good appetite*, reads a notation on the orphanage documents. In seven days, she would have nursed the infant dozens of times, bathed her at least once or twice, tended to her raw umbilical stump, dressed her and swaddled her, rocked her to sleep, gazed for hours into her dark, as yet unfocused eyes.

If the baby cried when she walked away, her breasts wept milk.

Every father of a family, or housekeeper, is required to affix a writing to the door of his house, specifying the name of each individual of his family, whether male or female, as well as the number of his horses. When any person dies, or leaves the dwelling, the name is struck out, and upon the occasion of a birth, is added to the list. By these means, the great officers of the province and governors of the cities are at all times acquainted with the exact number of the inhabitants.

Paper, moveable type, chopsticks, porcelain, medicine, the mariner's compass, the kite, the abacus, gunpowder, the multi-stage rocket. As any seventh grader can tell you, the list of inventions that China boasts is long and impressive. The Chinese may or may not have invented bureaucracy, but they embraced it early and practice it with zeal. In November 2000, shortly after we returned to North America with our daughter, they conducted their fifth official census since the birth of the People's Republic in 1949. Five million pollsters set out by bicycle, by car, and on foot and knocked on the doors of an estimated 350 million homes, asking a series of twenty-one detailed questions. How old are you? What is your ethnicity? Do you have a toilet? Does it flush? Demographers eagerly awaited the results of this survey. The 1990 census found a population of 1.13 billion; the official population in 2000 was 1.29 billion and by 2005 was more than 1.3 billion. But the accuracy of the count is in doubt. Despite a media campaign assuring citizens that their answers would not be used against them, census takers found it difficult to secure cooperation. Early in the process, even the *People's Daily* acknowledged errors. One of the biggest challenges confronting pollsters was obtaining a precise count of China's migrant workers — peasants who have fled the countryside's exhausted land in search of work in the smog-choked cities. At least a hundred million of them scuff the dirt roads in their cotton shoes. Possibly two hundred million or even more. No one knows for sure. Their shoes leave soft prints in the dust — a slight wind can blow them away.

At all seasons there is in the markets a great variety of herbs and fruits, and especially pears of an extraordinary size, weighing ten pounds each, that are white in the inside, like paste, and have a very fragrant smell.

Julie A. Mannella, writing in a 1996 issue of *Pediatric Basics*, argues that the base notes or flavor principles of a cuisine may be transmitted to a fetus through its mother's amniotic fluid, and then later, through her breast milk. Infants may therefore show an early and marked preference for the flavors most associated with their culture.

Zhejiang is rice country. My daughter loves rice, cooked any way at all, but especially in a congee made with pork and shredded cabbage, flavored with ginger and garlic. Apart from rice, she rejects the bland. Bananas bore her. She turns her face away from the rubbery skim milk mozzarella that a friend's baby adores. She prefers broccoli mashed with scallions, or a parsnip and carrot puree. She likes sour apricot, bitter cress, sweet apple, pungent onion, salty soy. At a street stall in Beijing, I discovered one of her favorites — yam, roasted over coals until its skin turns black and its center softens to a sticky pulp.

Yam. Hardy enough to thrive in times of famine. China's poorest food.

Mao encouraged the people to procreate. A peasant himself, he believed that a strong China meant a big China. The results were disastrous. As early as 1956, Zhou Enlai was urging limitations on childbirth, but until the late 1970s, less sensible voices prevailed, and throughout the 1960s and early 1970s, many families had as many as five or six children. Meanwhile, rapid and badly planned industrialization was shrinking the arable landmass, already half that of the United States. By the time the Chinese government decided to get serious about population control, the situation was dire. Many officials and economists of that period would have been adolescents or young adults during the famines of 1958

Photo by Catherine Farquharson

to 1961. Then, an estimated thirty million people died of starvation brought on by crop failure due to the misguided agricultural reforms of the "Great Leap Forward." Half the casualties were children under ten. If you look at a population graph from the 1990 census categorized by age and sex, you will see that young adults aged twenty-eight to thirty-two form the waist of an hourglass. That is the cohort who were babies during the famine years. Against this background, the one-child policy came into being.

Beginning in 1979, couples were limited to one child. Women who became pregnant without permission were subject to forced abortion, even in the third trimester. Over-quota births were punished with heavy fines and sterilization. Over-quota children could not be registered for schools and did not qualify for other state services. And parents who flouted the rule lost valuable medical and housing subsidies.

Yet, the one-child rule was never *just* a one-child rule. From the beginning, members of minority groups were permitted two children. And later, while urban and suburban Chinese remained limited to one, the rule was relaxed for rural dwellers. For them, "two children, one son" became the norm. Moreover, the policy was not equally enforced. In some areas, women's menstrual cycles were posted in the workplace, and if they did become pregnant, they might be dragged from their houses in the dark of night and injected with drugs to kill the fetus. In other places, cadres looked the other way or imposed only minor penalties when they learned of additional pregnancies. Eventually, as economic conditions improved, wealthier families simply paid the fines and had as many children as they wanted.

Has the one-child policy worked? Opinions are mixed. Urban and educated Chinese generally support the rule as necessary for continued economic prosperity. But some Western analysts argue that the population would have stabilized on its own, and that nothing can justify the human-rights abuses that the policy gave rise to. For now, the Chinese government is biding its time and promoting family planning.

My husband and I met our daughter in a hot, humid, government hall. It looked more like a primary school gym being readied for a Christmas recital. Rows of red plastic chairs and grey Formica tables, bolted to the floor, faced a raised proscenium. Red and green lights dangled from the ceiling. Whirring fans failed to cool the air or muffle the cries of thirteen other babies. We were here to sign official documents as well as to see our daughter for the first time. All we knew about her was written in that short "History of Infants" provided by the Hangzhou Children's Welfare Institute. Could we trust the information there? Within minutes of our first glimpse of her, we would be required to dip our thumbs in red ink, make a thumbprint, and formally accept her as our own. No turning back.

We waited. And waited. And waited. She'll be here at 9, we were told. Then 10; 10:30 came and went. The minutes passed slowly. We drank the bottled water thoughtfully supplied by government officials. We crossed the road to our hotel to retrieve forgotten articles. We watched the other families with their babies and snapped photographs.

"There she is," Mark said at last.

"That's not her." She was the only baby left, the final arrival, and still I failed to recognize her. Could the fragile, alert-looking fairy of our referral photo have turned into this large and slack-faced child? I sought her eyes; they seemed expressionless. Suddenly someone thrust her into my arms. My muscles tightened beneath the unaccustomed weight. "Mama," people were saying. "Mama." We stared at each other. She did not struggle. She did not cry. Instead, she turned her gaze to my lapel and began to finger the brooch I had attached there, a small Canadian flag. Then, exhausted by a terror no doubt greater than my own, she slept.

In their domestic manners they are free from jealousy or
suspicion of their wives, to whom great respect is shown . . .

Respect is a relative term. Conditions for women were hardly advanced in Marco Polo's Venice. And throughout history, women in China have fared even worse than they fared in other countries. For centuries, Chinese men, from the loftiest philosopher to the humblest servant, were united in their sense of superiority over the opposite sex. Confucian society was patrilineal — control of the land and all property passed from father to son. In return, a son worked the land or continued in the family business, ensured that the ancestral spirits were properly worshiped, and cared for the parents in their old age. In many families, a daughter was perceived as nothing more than an extra mouth to feed. "Girls are maggots in the rice," goes an old folk saying. When daughters married, their names were struck off their own family ledgers and entered into their husbands'. From cradle to grave, women were expected to obey: in childhood, their fathers; in youth and middle age, their husbands; in widowhood, their sons. A woman's highest purpose was to produce a male heir. And despite changes in the political system and a slow improvement in attitudes toward women, in a land where social security remains a dream for most, sons are still required.

Names matter. They matter especially to parents, for by naming, we express our dreams and desires, and declare a child our own. But adoptive parents of Chinese children ask themselves not only, "What shall we call her?" but also, "What has she been called — and by whom?" We wait by the phone with pen and paper and ask for a translation, or with characters in hand, we call up a Chinese-English dictionary on our computers and try to make sense of what we see. Zhen Juan (Precious and Beautiful). Qing Yuan (Clear Spring). Xia He (Summer Lotus). Chinese names are often rich in poetic association, but for English speakers they can be difficult to pronounce. Also, in most cases, orphanage officials, not birth parents, have decided what our children will be called. Even so, adoptive parents commonly retain these names. Whether they are actually used, they represent a link to the past. Sometimes, though, to preserve that link in a way that they can accept, parents must choose a Chinese name different from the one assigned. The translation of one daughter's name turned out to be Should Have Been Born a Boy.

If my daughter's birth mother named her, she kept that name a secret. Jinliang is the name the orphanage director chose. *Jin*, meaning gold, and *liang*, meaning virtuous or good, together connoting someone who is excellent or outstanding. Good as gold. Maia is the name we added. From the Sanskrit: creative power. From the Aramaic: water. From the Latin: springtime, growing. From the Greek: mother.

All over the world, all through history, hard times have led to infanticide. But few places on earth have known hard times like China's, or documented those hard times as China has. And when babies have been killed in China, overwhelmingly, they have been girls. During the early years of the one-child policy, female infanticide, having been almost unknown for years, began again in earnest. The practice was condemned by the state but, as Jonathan Spence notes in *The Search for Modern China*, "the very harshness of the critique hinted at the scale of the problem, believed by some Western analysts . . . to be in the region of 200,000 female babies a year." How do they die? They are plunged head first into ice water at birth, left on hilltops in hot weather, or smothered in bedding, their cries silenced. In one Anhui village alone, forty girls were drowned between 1980 and 1981. For families with money and education, a more palatable option is available. The new technologies of ultrasound and amniocentesis allow couples to identify the sex of a child before birth. International Planned Parenthood estimates that despite laws that forbid sex screening, 500,000 to 750,000 unborn baby girls are aborted every year.

The result is a serious population imbalance. A natural population ratio is about 105 boys to every 100 girls; in China today, there are 120 boys for every 100 girls. A 2000 census records nineteen million more boys than girls aged 0–15. Already, the effects of this are evident. Stories about the abduction and sale of women percolate in the *hutongs* (alleys) and on the news; even the government has acknowledged the problem. On the boardwalk in Hangzhou, I saw scores of toddlers clinging to their parents' shirttails. I can count the girls I saw on my fingers.

The stranger leaning over the baby carrier's rim at Guan Yin's shrine was not the only person who questioned my friend and me about our adoptions on the day we visited Lingyin Si. Later, as we wended our way through the shaded stone paths toward the exit, a crowd drew round. Amid the coos and sighs of the women, a young man's voice rang out, clear and emphatic: "Why do you adopt a Chinese baby?"

How to answer that question? Should I tell him about my desire to parent a child, my years of infertility, the decade or more I might wait to adopt an infant in my own country or my long-standing interest in Chinese culture? Here, in this ancient garden, surrounded by hundreds of Chinese, in the midst of a thriving city I might never have heard of had I not adopted this child, my "interest" was exposed as pitifully undeveloped.

I could not read his tone. Was he suspicious, even hostile? I had heard that some Chinese mistrust the motives of foreigners who adopt, fear that these children will be mistreated in their new homes. Did that kind of doubt lie behind his question? Since my arrival in China, no one had come closer to challenging me.

And if it was a challenge, it was not the first I had faced. Some people argue that it is never in the best interests of a child to remove her from the country and culture in which she was born. They argue that the practice of international adoption discourages sending countries from doing more to find solutions to the social problems that give rise to the pool of adoptable children within their borders. They argue that whatever safeguards and regulations are put in place, international adoption amounts to nothing more than relatively rich people taking children away from relatively poor people. And then there are those — legion in our society — who, deep in their hearts, see adoption as an inferior way to form a family. I hear their voices in supermarkets, at the playground, even in my living room. "Such a *kind* thing you are doing," they say. Or, "What do you know about her *real* mother?"

According to a Chinese folktale, an invisible red thread connects lovers who are destined to meet. The thread may tangle or stretch, but it can never be broken. Adoptive families have embraced this story to explain the uncanny bonds we often feel with our children — the way, from our first shared moments, we recognize them as our own. After a week in our daughter's company, Mark joked, "She likes to eat, and she likes to talk. She's come to the right family."

Whatever the rights or wrongs of international adoption, even its critics would acknowledge that it is far from the most exploitive practice perpetrated by the rich West. A few years ago, the *Washington Post* published a story about blood harvesting in

China's Anhui province. Anhui is poor and isolated, so its gene pool is unusually stable, making it a rich source of scientific data. But traditional Chinese beliefs militate against the donation of blood, so even the poorest peasant requires incentives to give it away. In this particular project, Harvard professors and Chinese government officials promised desperately needed health care in exchange, care that participants claim was never delivered. Instead, unbeknownst to them, their DNA was being collected to help multinational drug companies in the West develop new products. The blood is banked in university and company labs, a resource for future study; meanwhile, the peasants themselves are no healthier, no wealthier, no better off at all. Yet, if this story is true, their loss may turn out to be a gain for still another population, one entirely overlooked by researchers and participants alike. The "invisible red thread" that adoptive parents talk about may be visible, after all. Someday, for the thousands of children adopted in Anhui, that banked blood may lead back to their "real" mothers.

"Why do you adopt a Chinese baby?" The young man's expression was dignified and serious. His was not an idle question. He deserved an honest answer. But what to say? I looked at my daughter, still sleeping. Her head was tipped back. Her cheeks were softer than a peony blossom. Beneath their closed lids, her eyes briefly fluttered and then fell still. "Because we love her," I said at last. He smiled broadly then, and gave me the thumbs up.

Lingyin Si, the Temple of the Soul's Retreat, stands facing a beautiful hill, called Feilai Feng, "The Peak that Flew from Afar." The mountain is famous for its limestone carvings, in particular, one of a laughing Buddha. Many are restorations, but tourists in search of original work can climb the steep stairs cut into the rock face and search amid the nooks and crannies. When we visited, our tour guide recommended one such walk. Wearing the baby in the sling, and oppressed by the heat, I felt unable to make the climb, so I stood below while Mark went on with the camera. Workers were harvesting ginkgo, and the rattle of nuts and their peculiar stink permeated the air. Our daughter woke, and I bent my face toward her, babbling in the lilting tongue of mothers and babies everywhere, oblivious to my surroundings. The world shrank to a small point — the tip of her nose; expanded to an ocean's depth — the orbs of her eyes. I looked up at last to find us surrounded. Half a dozen young women crowded around, giggling and flipping their hair. When they saw that I had noticed them, they squeezed closer. Their boyfriends stood apart, taking pictures of them with the baby and me.

"Do you think they pray only for boys?" my friend had asked me earlier, as we watched the young woman bowing to Guan Yin. And yet, that morning on Feilai Feng, my daughter was dressed in pink.

Abandoning parents are understandably reluctant to talk about what they have done, so little is known for sure about their circumstances or their motives. But research has begun. In fieldwork conducted in Hunan and published in *Population and Development Review*, Kay Johnson, Huang Banghan, and Wang Liyao made some interesting discoveries. The typical abandoning parents in their study were average in almost every respect: A married couple in their mid-twenties to late thirties, with an average income for their area and an average level of education. In fifty percent of the cases, the husband made the decision to abandon, in forty percent of the cases it was a joint decision, and birth mothers alone decided in a further five percent. In-laws or other family members decided in the remaining cases. The typical abandoned child was "a healthy newborn girl who has one or more older sisters and no brothers. . . . Although many people abandon female infants in their quest to have a son, most do so only after they have reached or exceeded the limits imposed on them by birth planning."

The week she turned one, my daughter spoke her first English words: "boot" and "up." I like to think that the coupling may foretell something about her character: feet firmly on the ground, but arms stretched to the sky, the better to catch her dreams. In the months and years since then, she has learned to walk, to run, to play pretend, to speak in complex sentences, and to ask innumerable questions, including questions about her adoption. Her birth mother witnessed none of these milestones; her birth mother cannot offer answers.

Lingyin Si is only one of Hangzhou's many attractions. The city is also renowned for its fine silks, its Longjing tea, its beautiful lake — and its beautiful women. One million of them walk the causeways and ride the barges in the evenings with their husbands and boyfriends. They stamp documents, ring up sales, teach classes, diagnose illnesses, wait on tables, harvest rice. They vacuum the floors, straighten the sheets, and assemble the portable cribs in the five-star hotels where Western adoptive families stay.

One million. Three million in the greater metropolitan area.

It is the custom in [Hangzhou] with the indigent class of the people, who are unable to support their families, to sell their children to the rich, in order that they may be fed and brought up in a better manner than their own poverty would admit.

No trace.

The soul retreats in the face of mystery like this.

This Child of Mine

Denise Davy

IT WAS A WARM FRIDAY NIGHT in March. My teenage son
Ryan and I were standing on our front porch. He was wearing his
usual teenage uniform — baggy jeans, oversized T-shirt, and baseball cap. I was trying to convince him he needed a jacket, but the
unseasonably warm temperatures had him insisting otherwise.

He was heading out to meet friends at a local Tim Hortons
and was determined he didn't need a coat. I was determined he
did. I'd always hated the thought of him being cold, and now that
he was a teenager it was even more of a challenge to get him to
dress sensibly.

He finally relented and put on his oversized navy Wind River
sweatshirt. I kissed him on his cheek, the way I'd done a million
times before, and watched as he headed down the driveway. He
looked back at me and smiled the way he always did, half embarrassed, half liking it.

"Home by midnight," I said, as I waved goodbye.

It was around midnight when I awoke to a knock. I rushed downstairs, figuring Ryan forgot his keys. Instead, I made out the shadowy but unmistakable figures of two police officers. My stomach clenched.

I took a deep breath and opened the door.

"Do you have a son named Ryan?" one of them asked.

I let them in. They looked uncomfortable and exchanged uneasy glances. Then, one began to talk. A large group of teens had gathered for a bush party at a local soccer park. There'd been a lot of alcohol. Around 11 p.m., one boy wandered over to the railway tracks and fell into the path of an eastbound freight train.

My stomach clenched. I knew where they were going with the story. I'd heard it before when I covered the police beat. But in my world, those tragedies only happened to other people. The officer listed items they found at the scene: maroon watchband, jeans, baseball cap.

"Yes," I said, "but that could be anyone."

"Did he have braces?" asked the officer.

"He had a wire retainer."

"Did he have an asthma inhaler in his pocket?"

A chill went through me.

"I think I'd better call my father," I said, jumping up.

My father lived a block away. He arrived in minutes. I still remember how he almost collapsed when the officers told him they had reason to believe Ryan had been killed. He kept shouting, "No, no, no!" I was angry at him for believing them so readily and ran upstairs to find Ryan's dental X-rays and the fingerprints from the Child Find booklet. I gave them to the officers and they headed out the door to the hospital.

I knew that once they checked them they'd realize they'd made a terrible mistake.

The officers left. My father phoned my mother and gave her the news. We sat in the living room numb. No one spoke. Part of me knew the officers were right. My son was dead and I'd never see him again, but I couldn't accept it. I went into a state of shock that stayed with me for days.

During those days there was so much to do — all the funeral arrangements, writing the obituary, picking out a burial plot. I was in such a bewildered state and wanted to do everything right for my son, but at the same time I still didn't believe he was gone. I remember walking through the rows of coffins thinking, how do you choose a coffin for your only child?

I got through the days by putting one foot in front of the other and by relying on every survival strategy I'd ever learned in life. I was floating on a cushion of shock, still clinging to the possibility a mistake had been made. How could my son, who had been the center of my life for almost nineteen years, suddenly be gone? It was unimaginable.

My life and Ryan's had been a single braid. I'd raised him on my own since he was six months old. His father and I had separated and there were no visiting rights.

I'd watched him sprout from a three-and-a-half-pound premature infant into a handsome six-foot-three-inch young man with size twelve feet.

For more than eighteen years, our lives were wrapped around each other in a relationship unique to single parents. We'd been through the colicky nights, the emergency ward visits for his asthma attacks, the teacher interviews, the trip to Tokyo where he entertained the Japanese during our rides on the subways, and our famous wrestling matches.

We'd always wrestled, leaving the house looking like a hurricane zone. Living with Ryan, I would joke with him, was like living with Cato from the Pink Panther movies. I played Inspector

Clouseau. When he wasn't jumping out of closets at me, he was charging at me from across the room.

Our wrestling matches always finished with us laughing till we cried. Ryan had a definite gift for making people laugh. Friends were important to him and he valued them more than anything.

He took time to be with people, and friends told me he always knew the right thing to say when someone was down. As a result, he had a wealth of friends. For many of those friends, our home was their second home and was often filled with the voices of teenagers, their video games, and their music.

They'd visit after school and on weekends and empty my fridge of chicken nuggets and plum sauce. They'd sleep on the couch and family room floor and rise late the next day to play more video games. At times I wished they'd find another spot, but at the same time I loved it that they felt comfortable in our home. After all, I always knew where Ryan was.

It was spring and Ryan was preparing for a new chapter in his life. He was to head off to college to study broadcast journalism in September. Now, suddenly, he was gone.

In one second, I lost both my son and the right to call myself a mother. The teenage laughter in the house was gone, as was the sound of video games. For the first few weeks, none of it seemed real. But as the weeks wore on, the reality began to sink in and so began my journey into grief. I became more and more incapacitated, to the point where I couldn't eat or sleep or concentrate on anything for more than a few seconds.

I was exhausted and running on empty. I took up smoking after finding an old pack of cigarettes in Ryan's room. I hadn't smoked since high school, but within a week I was smoking a pack a day.

Friends and family became my lifelines. They brought me casseroles and homemade soups, scented candles, and healthy salads. They drove me to the cemetery and stayed with me through the night. People I'd never met, but who knew me from my work at the *Hamilton Spectator*, reached out with cards and letters.

Each act of kindness helped me get through another minute. Ryan's friends visited by the dozens and became my most precious lifelines. I'd sit with them and reminisce about the funny things Ryan did. Teenagers were so much more honest with their grief than adults.

They'd laugh and cry and hold each other when they needed someone to hang on to. They loved my son dearly, and their emotional honesty was a refreshing reminder to me of how special he was. His friends made up many of the 400 people who came to the funeral.

They were from high schools all over Burlington and cut across all lines. Boys and girls, young and old. Ryan was like that. No boundaries, no rules, as long as they knew how to laugh. I was fortunate in that my supervisors at the *Spectator* never pressured me to return to work. In fact, they insisted I take the time I needed to heal, paid for a yoga instructor to come to my home to teach me stress-reduction exercises, and even covered the cost of a Chinese dinner on my first Mother's Day. I counted on my friends to get me through each day, especially as the pain deepened. But while many encircled me with caring, there were others who added to my pain. They'd visit, then say cruel, hurtful things, or ramble on about their own problems.

Others, some of whom I considered my closest friends, disappeared without a trace. I tried to understand their absence. I knew I wasn't easy to be with, but I was too disabled with grief to teach anyone how to be with me. I learned later this was a common experience among bereaved parents.

"Losing your child is the true litmus test of a friendship," one bereaved parent told me.

Those people who stuck by me taught me about the true meaning of friendship, but even my best friends had to go home sometime. And when they did, a horrible silence came over the house. All those things I'd taken for granted were gone — his voice on the phone, his laughter, the shuffling of his baggy jeans when he walked down the hall, the smell of his Old Spice deodorant, the constant beep-beep of his video games.

There were times when I felt like I was on fire. Sometimes I felt panicky and out of control. I was coping one minute and the next I couldn't breathe. I would hyperventilate and run from room to room, unable to catch my breath.

Grief, I learned, was extremely physical. The pain was so intense, I felt like I'd come off an anesthetic halfway through an operation, still cut open and bleeding. I couldn't handle loud noises, even the sound of windshield wipers. Watching TV was impossible because of the constant images of violence. And every love song on the radio reminded me of Ryan.

It seemed every time I went into a store, I heard LeAnn Rimes singing, "How do I live without you?" Even carrying on a conversation became difficult. I'd forget simple words, fumble about like a stroke victim, then give up. Before the accident I juggled a demanding career, single parenthood, and caring for my home. Now making a cup of tea was an effort.

I was proud of my photographic memory, which had served me well as a reporter. Now, there were times I couldn't remember my own phone number. Many times I felt helpless and ready to give up, but another part of me, the fighter, was determined to make it through.

I was exhausting my friends and knew I needed to reach out for help. I started reading bereavement books, but I found them too clinical. Then I began searching for a bereavement counsellor. I knew from my research as a reporter that the counselling business is problematic. Anyone can hang up a shingle and call themselves a counsellor, so it's buyer beware.

Most counsellors I met were kind and gentle hand-holder types but knew little about the process of grieving or, more important, how to help me heal and move forward. Then I met Lori and Tony Antidormi. Their two-and-a-half-year-old son Zachary had been stabbed to death by a mentally ill neighbor. The date of Zachary's death was March 27, 1997, exactly one year before Ryan died.

The couple had not only survived the loss of their only child, but the pain of a high-profile court case and subsequent inquest. Lori wrote to me and offered her support and I gladly accepted. She and Tony helped me understand that time does heal wounds and assured me I would someday feel my spirit again.

I found hope, not only in their words, but in seeing people who had rebuilt their lives and found new joy. We kept in touch, visiting and phoning. About a year and a half after my son died, I experienced a dramatic turning point. I woke up one morning and felt a lightness so acute it was like I'd come out of a tunnel.

I believe I had simply bottomed out on grief. I'd indulged in it, cried, talked it out, acted it out, smoked my brains out. It was time to come back. I still weathered my share of ups and downs, but after that I was moving forward. I eased back into work, set up a fitness routine, and eventually quit smoking.

Most important, I moved forward on plans to become a mother again. Within months of losing my son, I'd thought about adopting a child. I'd tasted the joys of parenthood and knew nothing was better. I missed those things that make parenting so magical — waking up to my son's laughter, teaching him to ride a bike, seeing his face on Christmas morning.

And I missed being part of something bigger than my own little world. Since the moment Ryan came into my life, I'd felt part of some universal community, one in which we were connected by a greater purpose, that of being a parent. Someone had mentioned the idea of adopting from China and advised me to look into it, partly because China allowed single people to adopt (this has since changed) and also because the children are fairly healthy and the adoption process is smooth.

I'd already met with a social worker and begun the paperwork to adopt a little Chinese girl. I'd also signed on with Open Arms to International Adoption to facilitate the adoption and received approval from the appropriate government agencies. Now it was time to take the most important leap — ask them to send my application to China.

I faltered. I didn't know if I could handle being a parent again. I questioned whether my heart would ever heal enough for me to fully give my love to another child. A close friend who had adopted three children and who stuck by me gave me the best advice of anyone.

"Just keep moving ahead," he said. "If it feels wrong when you get on that plane, you can always change your mind."

It was good advice. I moved ahead. On June 13, 2000, one day after my son's birthday, I received a phone call from Open Arms director Deborah Maw saying she had five photos and medical reports for a nine-month-old baby girl named Ling Zhu. "She's absolutely beautiful," said Deborah.

I tore into Toronto, bursting with anticipation. Deborah opened a file folder to reveal five photos of the little girl who was to be my daughter. I gasped. She had a beautiful moon-shaped angel face, rosebud lips, a soft fringe of dark hair. Her eyes held such intelligence, her sweet mouth held such promise.

I couldn't wait to hold her, but at the same time I was panic-stricken over whether I could give this beautiful child the life she deserved. There were still times when I felt crippled with grief. I

Photo by Scott Gardner, *Hamilton Spectator*

decided to heed my friend's advice and keep moving ahead.

Two months later, I boarded a plane with a friend and five other couples who also worked through Open Arms and we made the gruelling trip to the other side of the world.

After two long days of sitting in planes and airports, we arrived at the Novotel Hotel in the city of Hefei, province of Anhui. It was midnight and there was little time to recover. At 9 o'clock the next morning, we met in a conference room in the hotel. A few minutes later, a line of Chinese nannies walked into the room, each carrying a nine-month-old baby. The babies were all wearing identical blue sleepers.

I searched the little girls' faces to see if I could find my daughter. Suddenly, someone called out, "Ling Zhu." I rushed forward. Her nanny placed her in my arms. Her hair was pulled tightly into yellow butterfly clips so she didn't look like her pictures.

She felt small and stiff and not at all comfortable with this new person. I stroked her face and told her I was her forever mommy and that she would be coming to live with me in a country called Canada. An hour later, she fell asleep in my arms and I started to fall in love.

By the next day, it was clear she'd decided our partnership was going to work. She clung to me with a certainty that convinced me we were absolutely meant to be together. A few days after our meeting, she looked at me and said, "Momma." That sealed our union.

I named her Emma, which appropriately means universal healer, and kept her Chinese name Ling as her middle name to honor her heritage. Ling Zhu means bright pearl, which she most certainly is. There's a brightness around this child of mine that lights up a room like 100 fireflies.

I'll never meet the Chinese officials who matched us, but they clearly saw something in our eyes and knew we were meant to be together. Sometimes she seems wise beyond her years, perhaps because her journey here was a long one, as was mine.

I'll probably never meet her Chinese mother who was forced to give her up because of the government's one-child policy. But I think about her often. Maybe that's because I know the pain of losing a child. I wish I could scream out to her that her little girl is beautiful and healthy and safe and, most of all, that she is loved. I don't know if it would fill the pain of not having her in her arms.

Some people believe losing my son was part of a divine plan that led me to China to adopt my little girl. The randomness of such a tragedy is just too terrifying. They believe there must be some reason. The sad truth is, there's never a reason for losing a child.

Ryan was taken from this world too soon and a great many things were left undone in his passing. He'll never meet his little sister, but he did play a part in her becoming my daughter. He taught me about the joys of motherhood. Now my daughter is continuing his lessons.

I've told my daughter about her big brother and his beautiful smile, piercing blue eyes, and quick wit. When she's older, I'll tell her how much he loved roller coasters and chicken nuggets and video games. I'll tell her how much he loved his friends and how much they loved him back.

I'll keep his spirit alive so he can teach his sister about life. That's what big brothers are for.

Two Boys, Two Girls

Sonja Smits

"I'M GOING TO MEET my new daughter."

It was not my new daughter in the flesh. The paperwork about the baby who was to be our new daughter had just arrived. After explaining this to my friend, she gave me a quick hug for luck and I flew up the stairs from the gym.

My workouts at the gym were an integral part of my stress-management strategy as we waited those endless months for word from the other side of the world. Now news had finally arrived via our social worker.

My husband and I had settled on China as the best option for adopting our second and final child. (Our daughter Avalon had been adopted three years earlier from Western Canada.) There was just one drawback: We would never have a son. We knew thousands of girls had been adopted from China, but the adoption of boys was all but unknown.

The idea of being the sole male in the family, surrounded by his loving wife and soon-to-be two daughters, suited my husband just fine.

It was not fine for our daughter, however, when we broached the topic of a new child in our family.

"Oh good, I'm getting a baby brother."

"No, honey, you're getting a baby sister."

"No! A brother," she insisted, even after our awkward explanation about why only girls were adopted from China.

Avalon already had an imaginary brother. While this is not unusual, what was remarkable was the doggedness with which his presence was maintained.

Crayon drawings of her family included mommy, daddy, the dog, grandma, and . . .

"Who's this?"

"Michael."

"Who's Michael?"

"My brother."

She would return home from birthday parties with an extra treat for her brother. Other parents at school would ask what grade Avalon's brother was in. We would have to explain that there was no brother. Now we had to tell her that there would never be a brother.

I, on the other hand, eventually embraced the "two girls, no boys" concept. That was the household I grew up in. In many ways, it was a relief; I had no idea how to raise a boy. A girl was familiar territory.

Frantically weaving through the Toronto traffic on the way to the social worker's office, images tumbled through my mind. Avalon's outfits had been carefully stored away in anticipation of our new daughter. One dress in particular, a ridiculously expensive black-and-white French lace confection, had looked adorable on

Avalon with her Slavic eyes and curly brown hair. Now, I pictured it on her almond-eyed, raven-haired sister. I imagined my daughters as teenagers, exquisitely reflecting the East and the West, European culture and the ancient civilization of China. I imagined them valiantly carrying the flag of feminism and sisterhood across the globe, Avalon showing her little sister the way.

I hoped they wouldn't be too competitive with each other. What if one was smarter than the other? What if one was prettier than the other? How would I deal with that?

Seated across from the social worker, the sole witness at the unveiling of our family's future, I held my breath. My husband, whom I had been unable to contact, was out of town. The social worker took her time perusing the papers in front of her. Everything was fine, everything was normal. Well, there were a couple of things . . .

I wanted to rip the paper from her hands, to lay my eyes at last on the little girl who would be ours. However, as a veteran of countless assessments to determine my suitability as an adoptive parent, I had learned to moderate my actions and expressions, lest I jeopardize the adoption.

Following an interminable pause, she spoke. "It appears to be a boy."

"A boy?"

I was stunned. Many years of trying to start a family, including various fertility ("futility") treatments had taught us that nothing was guaranteed. Except for this: every piece of reference material, every piece of correspondence, every workshop on adoptions from China referred to girls. As a feminist, I was ready and willing, and indeed felt privileged to do my part and guide a precious girl to a victorious life, to turn around her destiny in a patriarchal world. I would be fearless in my mission; Joan of Arc would pale by comparison.

But a boy? A Chinese boy? How would I guide him? Who would be his role model? Where in popular North American culture are the Chinese boys and men? They are not on our magazine stands or television sets or movies screens, aside from playing the role of action hero/clown.

The social worker handed me a grainy, black-and-white, passport-sized photocopy of a photo.

He was the most beautiful boy I had ever seen.

"There is one more thing," said the social worker.

According to the one-page medical report which listed his height, weight, head, and chest circumference, under the heading "Defects" were the words "Congenital heart disease."

Panic washed over me. Florence Nightingale is not a natural fit. When my husband broke his leg in a car accident in Morocco (yes, I was driving), I managed to play the good nurse for a while. Long enough to get him out of Morocco, flown to England for surgery, and finally back home to Canada. But after three weeks, when my husband with the thigh-high cast asked for help getting his sock on, I snapped.

"Oh, do it yourself. Just use a hanger."

How would I ever manage to deal with a child who suffered from congenital heart disease?

But it was too late, I had seen his picture.

The heart surgeon we called reassured us that, should it be necessary, heart surgery on children is usually very successful. The social worker reminded me that the Chinese rules specified that families adopting a second child would be given a child with a medical condition or a special need. That condition could be something as benign as flat feet. Since sons are traditionally highly valued in China, she speculated that the baby's medical condition was perhaps exaggerated in order to be adopted by foreigners. However there was no way to know until the adoption was complete and he was home with us in Canada.

Driving away from the office, I put my hand to my face. My cheeks felt like they were burning. I looked in the rearview mirror and I saw they were flaming pink.

Desperate to share the news with my husband, I finally was able to contact him. I told him there was a bit of a surprise.

"Twins?" he guessed.

"A boy."

"A boy?"

"A boy. And I know what his name will be."

"Michael," he said.

A few months later, a perfectly healthy and happy Lian Michael, our son, is in his car seat, next to his sister. My husband starts up the car and we are about to drive away when from the back seat, Avalon pipes up.

"Mommy's a girl and I'm a girl. Daddy's a boy and Lian's a boy. Two boys, two girls."

She let out a long, contented sigh. All was right with the world.

About Margaret

Havard Gould

IT IS 3:30 IN THE MORNING in Nanning and Margaret is sleeping.

I am not, because I am thinking about her and what she needs and has not had in her life. Found at a gas station the day after she was born, she has lived for sixteen months in an orphanage.

Now she is beside my hotel bed, in the small blue crib, having another one of her great big sleeps, sleeps that start easily and end gently.

Sometimes there is a soft little snore. She is undisturbed by the constant construction, the endless traffic of this big city in a hurry.

She is small. Very small. And scared. Of everything.

She is afraid of toys. She doesn't understand the meaning of that soft blanket I keep giving her. She doesn't know what a cracker is or what to do with it.

She doesn't reach out for things because, I think, she has not had things to reach out for. When finally handed the cracker, she scratches at it in a puzzled fashion, breaking it apart, not thinking it could be food.

She hasn't had enough food. Her cheeks are chubby but her body is light.

There is a sad but hilarious official document detailing her daily habits. She apparently gets up at 6 a.m., usually, and eats four meals a day, the last one at midnight.

She goes to bed at 10, it says.

Perhaps they meant she has some formula at midnight. As far as I can tell, the only foods she recognizes are rice congee (a porridge) and formula.

I know the document is full of nonsense. It says Margaret is outgoing, always playing with friends.

Here is how I know this is nonsense. Her nanny knew better.

There was a ceremony for the newly adopted girls. A podium, flags, speeches, and gifts. And when it was over, down in the big, marble lobby, there were three women from the orphanage. A director, I think, and a supervisor, perhaps, two serious, official-looking women. And a fresh-faced twenty-year-old, shining with energy and enthusiasm.

She recognized Margaret. And Margaret recognized her.

It was the first time I saw Margaret reach out for anything. She wanted her nanny. Margaret was in her arms in a second.

The bus was leaving, we had to go.

But as Margaret clung to her past, I pulled out a tape recorder and tried to get her nanny to talk about Margaret's months in the orphanage.

The nanny knew the cliché, in English.

"Good girl," she said.

I motioned for more, in Chinese, please. Seeing the tape

recorder, she might have understood I was desperate for a glimpse through a doorway that was closing forever.

She spoke. I smiled, understanding nothing.

The translator who listened to the recording later told me about Margaret's life in the orphanage.

Not outgoing. Not surrounded by friends.

But shy. Quiet. Alone.

I am flattered that she now clings to me. Not alone, I tell her. Not ever again. She has a mother and two sisters and me. Alone isn't going to happen anymore.

Margaret has a serious air about her. She gazes at everything intently. Her head snaps about when there is a new sound to assess. But there is never any panic. Just calm curiosity.

I am not going to shorten her name to Meg or Maggie while we are here. She is too serious. She needs a big name. There is something about reducing the name of a child who has had so

Photo by Catherine Farquharson

little. It makes no sense, but she cannot be a Maggie or a Meg until there is a sense of fun.

She can't walk. Or crawl. I think she has been confined to a crib for long, long periods.

All the children had their own cribs. They slept alone, all the parents were told. They were bathed every day, twice a day in hot weather. That does not sound like long baths with playful splashing. And, of course, Margaret is afraid of the bath I give her. Silently fearful, her hands suspended above the water, eyes large, mouth closed.

Tonight, I am playing tricks, leaving a particularly interesting roll of yellow duct tape just outside her reach. Putting her in the doorway of the hotel room and backing away. To see if she will crawl to me. Or away.

She doesn't. She can't.

So she scratches at the roll of yellow duct tape she has been given. Cries softly to be carried (and stops immediately when she is lifted).

She is afraid of the high chair and the stroller. She whimpers. A soft sound as if she expects no response.

For the first twelve hours, she pouted. No spoon or bottle could get past her small, stubborn lips. She slept in fear, on her back, arms bent at the elbows, palms up as if to ward off the massive changes in her life.

But she relented. Formula in a bottle is acceptable to the small, serious one. Apple juice in a sippy cup is not wanted at this time.

She is open to further experimentation. Spaghetti met with her approval. Noodles are okay. Meat is not. A small bit of fried egg was welcomed.

But only when fed to her. She doesn't know how to pick it up with her hands. That ridiculous document says she likes to eat with her fingers. Yet she tried to lick noodles off a plate, her hands unused.

She won't shake her head to say no. When she is given a bottle she doesn't want, she sticks out her tiny tongue as the nipple approaches.

There is nothing wrong with her. I have stopped worrying. She is alert and learning.

Already, she has discovered that it is fun to slap the bottle while Dad holds it. And the fear of the finger puppet (a dog with a magician's hat) has been conquered. It has become faintly amusing to pick it up and throw it on the floor so Dad will get it. Endlessly, apparently.

But it's only faintly funny because she doesn't smile much. I have seen a couple. No laughter.

Out of the blue, she decided to stand at dinner tonight. And tried to walk, sort of. But no amount of cheering and applause could summon a grin from the stoic one.

Hugs are appreciated, I think. And tonight she wanted to climb on me on the bed to fall asleep, her face buried in my neck, her soft breath tickling me.

But she needs to learn how to laugh. She needs to hear her sisters Gwendolyn and Nell tell knock-knock jokes. She needs to see those kids play with blocks, hug their stuffed animals, roll toy trucks, and bounce balls. She needs to learn about fun and laughter and crying.

Yes, crying. She doesn't cry, much. Perhaps because she has been trained to expect that no one will come, scoop her up, and fix what is wrong.

She can change. She spent an entire half hour playing with a toy airplane, examining it, scratching it, bouncing it off the mattress. In an amazing burst of energy, she has become a mountain goat, trying to climb up Dad to get to his head to tug gently at his hair. But often she just sits and gazes, taking everything in. It must be exhausting for her. Without complaint, her eyelids become heavy and she is gone on my shoulder.

I put her in the crib late this afternoon, thinking she needed a second nap. She went without protest. But didn't sleep. Just studied the ceiling quietly, without a sound or a frown or movement.

She is responding, changing rapidly. And I repeat — I am not worried. Just glad that two files from opposites sides of the world have come together and she is ours. She is her own small self, though, with her placid reactions to wrenching events. And a little quirk: she crosses two fingers, as if wishing for good luck. Sometimes her little fingers turn white with the pressure.

It is too much to think about, her lying quietly in her orphanage crib, her fingers crossed in the long sixteen months before she was found again.

I will go back to bed again, for I must be ready to carry and cajole and trick Margaret into the childhood that, until now, has been denied.

This Baby's Going to Fly

Ann Rauhala

THERE IS SOMETHING SO PRESUMPTUOUS about naming a child. A name is not just a name, despite what Juliet said about flowers. Look where she ended up.

A rose by any other name may still be a rose, but will it be as velvety, as layered, as recognized for its sheer flowerhood if it is called a mugwump or a stinkweed?

I don't think so.

Naming our daughter was serious business. We'd been through the baby-naming drill with our son nine years before. We knew it was momentous, that it would influence how people would see him his whole life.

As we waited through that pregnancy, we'd toss ideas back and forth, making one list. Instinct told us to dwell more on the boys' names. My husband liked Elijah, but I recalled Cher's offspring by an Allman brother. Michael wasn't for us but we liked the more offbeat Mickey — not thinking, evidently, about Disneyland.

Rufus? Distinctive, yes, but what if the boy had a speech impediment?

My husband, the poker player, suggested Lucky.

Yes, perfect, I said, if he has adorable triangular ears and a taste for kibble.

As the due date drew near, we felt the pressing need for a short list. We reasoned that it was wrong to name him before we met him. That presumption again; the kid would be stuck with the name for eighty years or more. The least we could do is take a look at him first.

Still, we needed *some* agreement. We decided on David, Sam, or Mickey. Yes, Mickey. I still blame the hormones.

When the baby was born that humid June morning, Mickey didn't seem so farfetched. Apart from his resemblance to a gentle cartoon character, the boy had the look of a wiseguy about him. Mickey Spillane sprang to mind.

What he clearly was not was a David. He did not have the soulful look that I, for some reason, expected in a David. Instead, there was a cheerful, wisenheimer air about him. Let's pull a fast one, his expression said. He seemed to be winking even when he wasn't.

The truth was, he looked like a Sam — relaxed and ready with a quip. The name fit him like a newborn Pampers.

Nine years later we were at it again. This time, Sam, his father, and I sat in a hotel room in Hefei, the capital of the Anhui province in central China. We struggled to figure out what to call the bright-eyed baby girl who was plunked at our feet, playing with a luggage tag with all the absorption of Madame Curie examining a beaker of radium.

We just did not know. That seems to be unusual among adoptive parents. Most people have a name in mind months or even years before they take a baby into their arms. Dozens of Mings,

Wencis, and Bos exist as Charlottes, Jasmines, or Ashleys in the imaginations of their adoptive parents-to-be long before they're even born.

I understand. So many people come to adoption after a long, sad wait for a child. They have been consoling themselves with hopeful activities — thinking up names, painting nurseries, focusing on the future.

But we did not want to do that. We thought Sam had suited Sam, and so we stuck with what worked: Come up with a short list and then wait until we meet the candidate.

During the thirteen or so months of waiting, we had our nicknames for She Who Was to Be. A favorite was Ling, a nod to Ling-Ling, the panda that Zhou Enlai presented as a détente gift to Richard Nixon.

With breezy cultural insensitivity, we also called her Miss Plum Blossom. Another favorite was Little Sister, or Meimei, Mandarin for the same. But we never thought of her as Jennifer or Sarah or Rachel. We had to meet her before we named her.

Of course, there were many more variables this time around. For one thing, this baby already *had* a name, given to her by orphanage staff. We learned it from the agency the night before her pictures were couriered to us, part of what is known as the official offer to adopt. Her name was Ling Fei, a melodic name that tinkled like little wind chimes.

We laughed. It was uncanny. She was a Ling after all. We looked at her photo, over and over, our eyes blurred with tears. She's adorable, we thought, but nothing like a panda.

We scrambled to find clues about her Chinese name. All the babies from her orphanage, the Tongling Social Welfare Institute, were given the surname Tong or Ling. No mystery there. But the name Fei was unusual for a girl, a Chinese friend told us. Fei in this case seemed to mean flying.

Photo by Catherine Farquharson

Cool, Sam said. Not orchid or ruby or lovely, but *flying*.

The pictures showed a round-cheeked, clear-eyed girl with a high forehead, a bad haircut, and a look of steely intelligence. "She looks very determined," my mother said, a pronouncement we cite now as evidence of grandmotherly foresight.

Ling Fei, with the last name given first as the Chinese do. We liked its sound and its meaning, but had doubts about using it exclusively. We'd keep it as a middle name. If she wanted to be Ling or Fei or both later on, they were her personal treasures to use. But I wanted to give her a simple Anglicized name that she could wrap around her like Harry Potter's invisibility cloak, to let her blend in at the schoolyard.

I was always grateful that my parents named me Ann to balance out my multi-syllabic Finnish last name that, proud as I am of it, few could ever spell or pronounce on the first try. Belonging is one part being yourself and one part feeling at ease.

The photos of Ling Fei set off the short-list debate. So many perfectly good names had to go, what with nieces, cousins, and old rivals rendering them unusable. Goodbye Emily, Katherine, Alexandra.

I liked Robin; my husband hated it. He offered Carly; I thought not.

"What about Phoebe?" I tried. "She looks like she could pull it off."

Sam was quick to take up his duties as big brother. "Right," he said. "Why don't you just paint a target on her back?"

"But Daddy and I like it. It's cute. It's different."

He stood firm in Meimei's defence. "Too different."

Six weeks later we left for China with a short list: Julia, Annie, and Rosie. Like Sam, names that were unfussy, unadorned, and possible for a child to make her own.

Now, as we fidgeted in the hotel room, the naming moment

had come and we could only sputter. Amid cushions and toys, the baby sat smiling conspiratorially at her new brother — when she could tear her attention from that spellbinding Air China tag.

She didn't know that she didn't have her permanent name yet. She clearly responded to Feifei, the nickname the orphanage workers used. Feifei was a pleasing name that we would keep and cherish. But it wasn't the real deal.

I had arrived in China with a secret agenda to push the name Julia — an elegant name that I thought would suit this pretty baby. Princess-ify the family a little, I thought; first this, then the canopied bed. But this child's intense focus, the way she alone among the babies in our group did not even cry as she was handed over, made me ask: could the name Julia even begin to contain her?

She was not about to disintegrate into tears in front of some odd-looking foreigners. When we met, she smiled sparingly at us, beamed at Sam, and tried to wrest the video camera from my hands. Somehow she did not seem as malleable or delicate as a Julia ought to be.

Two hours later, back in our room, jet-lagged and hungry, we were in no condition to decide. We were in awe of this self-possessed little stranger whose life was now ours for safekeeping.

"I think Julia is out," I told the guys. They said nothing. They already knew it.

The next day, Feifei remained Feifei while we hoped for inspiration. We met up with the other parents in our travel group, most of them ecstatic and exhausted. Every other baby had a name. There were jokes about our indecision. That day and the next rolled by like a travel video on fast-forward, dazzling with sights and sounds.

Seventy-two hours passed and she was still "the baby." Or Lingy (rhymes with stringy). We had learned a lot about her. At eleven months she showed an incredible taste for everything within her grasp — and beyond. She ate and drank and eliminated almost twice as much as her Tongling teammates. While Katie or Rebekah or Emma nestled in parental arms, Lingy preferred standing or climbing or bouncing on laps or floors or tabletops. Plopped down for a minute on a carpet, she'd scuttle like a windup toy toward any stable vertical surface and pull herself to standing.

She loved to fly in our arms overhead. She loved flashing lights, flags and mirrors, cameras, curtain strings and electrical cords, rubber ducks, bottle caps and crinkly paper, bananas, pureed yams, and any beverage. Also the red sweater my mother knit for her. In no order at all and preferably simultaneously.

She loved sleeping, she loved waking up. She loved morning, noon, and night. In the hotel room, she liked to ride on Sam's back like a pint-sized cowpoke. It was looking like *Annie Get Your Gun*. So then, Annie?

Still. Annie was part of my name, although only my husband was ever allowed to use the diminutive. Could I give up this term of endearment to the upstart? Was there room in our household for two sharpshooters?

I began to argue furiously for Rosie. Likable, I pleaded, beguiling, fresh, innocent, can be shortened to Rose. I stopped to reload.

Sam didn't like Rose, he wasn't even sure anymore about Rosie.

"C'mon, c'mon. Rosie the riveter, symbol of proud, independent woman," I wheedled.

"Kinda reminds me of a clown," Sam said.

"He's got a point," my husband said. He preferred Annie.

I twisted and turned. I pretended to be considerate. What about our friend Annie, marathon runner, human rights advocate, wearer of size four? She won't appreciate being called Big Annie.

"She'll think it's funny," my husband said.

I thought about my extended family, of its many opinionated women, outspoken and outgoing. Thinking of the generations, I could not recall one person named Rose. Many were named Ann or Anna.

I thought about how Sam has two middle names, from great-grandfathers on both sides. I thought about how a mother connects a child to the past. I realized that, as unusual a choice as it might seem, sharing my first name with this daredevil of a girl was a bond I wanted to have.

Sam closed the case. "Annie is a happy name. And she's a happy baby."

Ling Fei's first name became Annie. She'll be eight next week. She says she's going to be an airplane pilot. Fei after all.

Carry Me

Jasmine Akbarali

ONE OF MY TWINS WANTS to be carried. I oblige her. I like carrying my daughters. I like the softness of their small arms encircling my neck. I like the weight of their heads resting against my shoulders, and the way their little breaths rhythmically warm my collarbone. Even as they grow bigger and heavier, and as carrying them becomes more laborious; even when they are messy and their dirty hands and feet smear my clothes; even when they insist on being carried together, with no thought to the strain on my lower back; even then I like to carry them.

It reminds me of the first time I held their small bodies in my arms, so slight, yet so overwhelming.

I first embraced my daughters when they were fifteen months old. Flanked by the Canadian and Chinese flags, my daughters' nanny, a young, pretty woman with soft features and a big smile, handed me my older child. I was overcome with joy, but my daughter did not share my happy feelings. Almost immediately she began to cry, and it was weeks before she stopped. In that time, my husband and I faithfully carried her, convinced that through this shared physical contact, and through the cycle of meeting her arising needs, she would begin to love us.

My younger daughter was less cautious than her older twin. She was accustomed to working the room, playing up her dimples to her advantage. She was perfectly happy to be with us, or with anyone who would dote on her. She, too, we carried. We carried her partly to be sure she would not make off with some seemingly amiable person, but also to begin to cement in her the understanding that her relationship with us was different. Within a few weeks, she wanted to be carried only by us, and needed our physical presence to comfort her. For months, we carried her, constant in our belief that this physical reassurance would heal any mistrust that she still harbored.

When I carry my daughters, I am reminded of the women who cared for them before I was given the privilege. For many months, their sweet-faced nanny tended to them, and the way she held them displayed the ease with which their small bodies fit into her embrace. The last time she saw my daughters, she clasped my hand tightly, and through her touch, told me what I needed to know: she had loved my children well. Leaving them with me, she must have felt an emptiness where, not long before, there had been two small, wriggling bodies. I remember my daughters' nanny often, with awe and gratitude. She carried them when I could not, and did so with love, knowing how briefly these children would be in her life.

Thinking of that sacrifice and loss, I consider the first woman who carried them, for nine months, while her belly expanded. She is a mystery to me. I know nothing about my daughters' birth mother, but there is much that I wonder. Who is she? Does anyone call her "Mother"? Does she have the heart-shaped face my daughters wear? Does she share their artistic skill? Their love of music? I know my daughters better than anyone: the curve of their shoulder blades, the location of each mosquito bite, the meaning of each cry and each sigh. But of their beginnings, I

know nothing. Instead, I carry with me a list of questions about this woman. What did she feel as they grew inside her? What hope did she hold in her heart for her children? What did she suffer to let them go from her life?

We are mothers to the same children but only I have the joy of watching them grow. Does she wonder where they are in the world? Who they are becoming? Are she and I the only two who remember her loss? I do not judge her actions, but, equally, I cannot fathom them. My questions about her grief burden me, as her grief must burden her. I stand with her, bound to her, for her sorrow is a weight we both must bear.

I sense her presence in my family, and was surprised to realize that I mourn her absence — for my daughters but also for me. Like borrowed shoes, I wear this grief awkwardly, and try to get comfortable in it. My daughters are beginning to comprehend what happened. To help them grieve their losses, I need first to find peace with my own. And with hers.

When I carry my daughters I connect myself to their earliest days, and to those people who protected them. Carrying them lightens my load. Several years have passed and my daughters have grown into "big girls." They are confident enough that they do not often need to be carried. Soon, they will not want to be carried at all, and not so long after that they may carry their own. But for now, when they come to me with outstretched arms, I will gladly put aside what I am doing to pick them up, hold them tightly, and reflect a moment on my tremendous luck to have found my way to my children. When the day arrives that I can no longer carry them in my arms, I am comforted by the knowledge that I will hold them close forever.

An Arranged Family

Julie Chan

MY DAUGHTER LOOKS VERY much a part of me. We both have large brown eyes, straight dark hair, and a similar complexion. At the age of two, she skirts around my legs, reaches out to hold my hand, and at every opportunity jumps into my lap for a cuddle. When I pick her up from nursery school, she runs into my arms, her face beaming. She calls me "Mama," and every day we tell each other "I love you." Along with my husband Jonathan, my Chinese daughter and I are a family.

I am Canadian but also Chinese. My parents and grandparents were born in China. With this ancestry, having a Chinese daughter should not be extraordinary. But it is.

My parents followed the classic model of Chinese who immigrated to Canada in the 1940s and 1950s. My father arrived in Canada as a young teenager and returned to Hong Kong in his twenties to find a wife. He brought his bride to Canada, where

Photo by Catherine Farquharson

he started a career as a restaurant owner and where my mom started life as a wife and mother. I'm sure that my parents hoped, as I was growing up, that I would marry a nice Chinese boy who could speak Chinese, understand Chinese culture, and — most important — love Chinese food.

And while there were many Chinese students in my schools and neighborhood, there were even more Italians, Portuguese, Greeks, Caribbeans, East Indians, and other Europeans. Given this broad ethnic choice of friends, the chances of my parents toasting a Chinese son-in-law or doting over a black-haired, rosy-cheeked Chinese grandchild were anything but guaranteed.

Not long after I got to an age when my parents were seriously concerned that I would be single for the rest of my life, I married an Englishman. Jonathan has blond hair, blue eyes, pale skin, and speaks only English. Since my only sibling married an Australian, it looked like our family was not destined to have those Chinese grandchildren.

But my parents' dreams became a reality, after all. In 2002, my husband and I adopted Emma. She is black-haired, brown-eyed, rosy-cheeked, and delightful. I had become the mother of a Chinese daughter.

At the time of our adoption, the China Center of Adoption Affairs favored adoptive parents of Chinese origin. I provided my parents' birth certificates to prove that our adopted daughter would have authentic "born in China" grandparents. With this, we were put on the fast track. We waited only five months for a referral while non-Chinese families waited almost three times longer. It is rumored that Chinese officials would provide Chinese families with the best-looking and healthiest children. I cannot verify this but I can say that Emma is thriving and to us is the most beautiful little girl in the world.

As we prepared to meet our daughter, Jonathan and I decided that I would be the first to hold her. He thought she might react negatively to a pale, fair-haired man. We thought perhaps my Chinese face and a few words of recently learned Mandarin would put her more at ease.

When I first met Emma, I was filled with emotions — excited to meet her but exhausted from the long physical and emotional journey to China. When I took Emma from her caregiver's arms, she did not cry, but looked tired and unsure. In my mind, I blocked out the noise and movements of other families meeting their children. This was our private moment. I held Emma and kissed her gently. Her cheeks were red, warm, and chubby. Then Jonathan held Emma for most of the three hours we spent at the administrative office while I managed the adoption paperwork. A wonderful thing started to happen. Emma looked into Jonathan's eyes, and hardly took her eyes off him. No smiles, no expressions, just gazes. In return, he spoke to her quietly, looked at her lovingly, and gave her gentle kisses. They were beginning to fall in love.

In some respects, my daughter's journey to Canada echoed my mother's, each of them a girl leaving China behind to pursue a better life and a better future. My mother was introduced to my father through their parents and other interested relatives who saw them as a good match. It was much like an arranged marriage. Emma was introduced to me and my husband through a third party, and ours became an arranged family.

My mother's father, husband, and relatives welcomed her entry to Canada. Although my mother's new homeland was Canada, her new life was filled exclusively with Chinese relatives and culture. Maintaining the old ways was essential to her feeling comfortable and secure in a land so different from China.

When Emma came to Canada, she, too, got a warm welcome

from our families and an extended network of friends. But unlike my mother, Emma was quickly immersed into the Canadian way of life. She had lessons in swimming, music, ballet, and gymnastics, and attended nursery school.

My daughter's and my parents' experiences are not so different from the immigration of our Chinese ancestors. In the late 1890s, Chinese came to North America or "Golden Mountain" as they called it, to find a place of freedom and prosperity. They hoped to become rich in the gold rush. Very few struck gold but many stayed on to work in factories and in laundries or make a living by fishing or farming. "Golden Mountain" has come to mean a land of opportunity for Chinese immigrants. My daughter may have arrived more than 100 years after the first Chinese, but she, too, came for a life with more opportunity.

Along with these parallels, there is this paradox: most Chinese immigrants to Canada 100 years ago were men who were often forced into lifelong bachelorhood by Canadian laws restricting the immigration of women and families. Today's baby girls are leaving behind a China which seems very likely to face its own surplus of lonely bachelors.

I rely on my parents to teach me my heritage, and through them, Emma is given an appreciation of her Chinese background. Even though she left China as a baby, I believe that Emma "feels" Chinese. At a hearing test, the audiologist said Emma has a preference for the lower tones more prevalent in Chinese. Tofu, dim sum, homemade Chinese soups, noodles, and rice are her favorite foods. When we gather with my relatives, Emma fits right in, running in a pack with all her little cousins. When we are together as a family, no one singles her out as "adopted." Having a Chinese mother and family means Emma can more easily protect her privacy than Chinese children adopted into non-Chinese families.

Emma visits her Chinese grandparents once a week on what we call "pohpo" day. Every Friday, Emma declares, "I love *pohpo* day!" When she arrives at my parents' house, Emma runs to them with "Hello, *pohpo*" and "Hello, *gunggung*." They speak Cantonese to her and my mother serves up delicious Chinese food. Emma tucks into dishes like fried rice, noodles, and her favorite "cha sui baus" or little BBQ pork buns. She slurps up noodles, chews on chicken drumsticks, and sips her soup right out of the bowl. Emma has learned many Chinese words from her grandparents. She counts to ten, labels many food items and politely says "*dòjeh*" for thank you.

As I watch Emma with my parents, it reminds me of my special relationship with my own grandparents. My visits with them reinforced my ability to speak Chinese. At my parents' house, I'm delighted to hear Emma speaking Chinese and exclaiming the occasional "*Ai Ya!*"

While my parents maintained a relatively traditional Chinese household, they did not insist on my learning every custom. At home, we ate Chinese foods — which I love — but my mother sent me to school with ham sandwiches made with Wonder bread and Campbell's chicken noodle soup. Each year, I was feted on two birthdays. For my birthday according to the lunar calendar, my parents gave me a large chicken drumstick for dinner and a red envelope of lucky money. On my other birthday, I got a cake with candles and invited all my friends from school. We also held two New Year's celebrations, one on December 31, and the other on the Lunar New Year, which always seemed to be in the coldest part of winter.

My spoken Chinese is good, but it is the dialect of my parents' village in China, not the more popular Cantonese or the more universally spoken Mandarin. My parents did not send me to Chinese classes but instead to private music lessons at the Royal

Conservatory of Music. We did not vacation in the "homeland" but in New York on Coney Island Beach, where we spent summers visiting my grandparents. My parents wanted me to have the best of both worlds, maintaining some degree of Chinese heritage while being, at heart, a Canadian.

Now that I have a Chinese daughter, I have become more interested in my cultural roots. Without the adoption trip, I would not have taken Mandarin classes. I've hosted my first Chinese New Year's dinner and already started teaching my daughter how to cook Chinese at wonton-making parties at my parents' house. She delights in taking the wonton skins and pinching them up into little purses.

The girls who have left China have become ambassadors for the land where they were born. By sending its girls around the world, China is spreading its culture across the globe. These girls have opened up an awareness of and appreciation for Chinese culture and its people. I have never seen so many non-Chinese embrace Chinese culture so warmly.

At the annual New Year's dinner near Toronto hosted by Families with Children from China, more than 700 people feast on a multi-course banquet and cheer on a noisy lion dance. Most of the kids are Chinese girls, while most parents are white.

Last winter, we visited a non-Chinese family with adopted Chinese girls. Their house was decorated for the Lunar New Year, with large red Chinese characters for good luck on their front door. Inside, they had Chinese souvenirs and art work all around the house. Their kids wore closely fitted and high-collared Chinese dresses and the mother wore a Chinese jacket. Looking around, I felt a little strange. They seemed more Chinese than me!

I will never know firsthand the issues related to having a child of a different culture or "look" than me. But I do know that Emma won't need to go far to experience Chinese culture. Growing up in Canada, she will embrace multiple cultures and heritages. They will provide her with a richer life and a better appreciation of the differences in people and their ideas. She will be a Canadian but will learn English traditions from her father and English grandmother. Through her Chinese grandparents, she'll learn Chinese customs and language. Through me, she'll learn to blend it all together, to be proud of who she is.

I hope that some day China will invite all their little ambassadors to visit. My daughter won't forget China; I hope China will never forget her.

Hua Jun Gets Daddy

Douglas Hood

AT A DINNER PARTY RECENTLY I mentioned taking Suki to her first movie, *Pocahontas*. Someone said, "Did you notice they really did up Pocahontas, with a push-up bra and tight skirt?" I answered, "Actually, I found her girlfriend cuter, with her little bangs and all." Another friend lowered his voice and said, "Doug, it's just a cartoon."

"Listen, you're not a single guy raising a four-year-old daughter."

I was forty-six years old, decidedly single, and the details of my life were worked to near-perfection: weekends at a lake cabin, marathons, hopping planes to Paris or Buenos Aires. In a bizarre twist, the last thing I needed actually became my obsession — a child. I pursued adoption, was shocked to find I qualified, and dreadfully closed in on the ultimate commitment. In my head, I played out many of my concerns — would I give up my *New Yorker* for *Curious George*, forgo running for coloring, tend to another's potty instead of my own quads, and put up with spittle on my shirt and spilled milk on my computer? I would, I thought.

But was I willing to let a communist bureaucrat select my child from his orphanage?

A one-inch photocopy arrived from the other side of the earth, a puffy, pouty face. For weeks I studied it, propped it up on the dinner table and, over my speedometer, talked to it, and pretended I loved this girl named Hua Jun. I strained to imagine her smiling, one day pretty, and frolicking with me, splashing me with hugs and kisses. But lurking in my mind I could hear the future matter-of-fact voices of my friends, "Doug had a near-breakdown from having to cope with a little ADD pyromaniac from China."

At Hangzhou they handed over four-year-old Hua Jun, undersized and floppy, with only the shirt (and bug bites) on her back. She was a peasant, abandoned at a train station. I called her Suki and handed her an apple. Ten minutes later she tapped my arm and returned the stem. One inch of stem, nothing more. Her first word was the one I thought I'd never hear, "Papa."

There's no mama at our home. And I'm no substitute. Instead of folding her dresses, we stash them in a drawer and flap our arms to Madonna in the living room. Instead of watching *Sesame Street*, we paint her face with Caran d'Ache and ride the bike, waving and weaving through the neighborhood. I drop her off at preschool draped in old-fashioned jewelry and a Boston Red Sox cap. I put a number seven on her cheek when Mantle dies. Instead of making sand cakes, we grit our teeth, shiver, and swim across the lake. We park the truck and jog through the woods, get home after dark, down a thick shake, and trade burps. We wear sweats to bed and one of her first words is "sweaty." All right, her buttons should be in front and my socks don't match — but hey, you should have seen our soccer match in the backyard.

We'd love to have a mom. I could send her in my stead to some of the places I can't believe I go: Chuck E. Cheese, Jennifer's birthday party, and showers — and I don't mean the ones where Suki pulls open the curtain on me. The baby kind. I've racked up five. I'm hanging with mommies, wiping snot with my finger, and talking about pull-ups, kindergartens, and spot removers.

Mothers tell me there's more; take her to Discovery Zone and Dairy Queen, to the zoo, to the library. But I toss her a globe, point to Myanmar and Tegucigalpa, and tell her: anywhere, anytime. I pat the big ball and say, "Suki's." I've got four decades on her and a drawer full of maps. But I can't shake her off my thigh. I talk on the phone and she's got me in a Peking neck twirl. I wake in the morning because her foot is in my face. I go to the bathroom, the door cracks and I see an eye. Finally I see, she's got her world.

I talk to mothers. When I'm asked, "Where is the cutie today?" I slap my head and say, "Oh God, I left her in the car!" Or just today I was asked, "Have you decided on a school?" I said, "I'm thinking of Spring Glen, but I'm bugged by her walking the mile home alone in the dark." Just kidding, just kidding.

I talk to my new daughter: "Suki, get your hand out of there!" (Urinal.) "Don't pull that!" (Fire alarm.) "Don't turn that!" (Ignition while we're on the George Washington.) "Do you have *Ultimate Fighter*?" (Us at Blockbuster.) "Play hurt!" (She falls.) Or: "Yukka!" (Picks nose, wipes on Papa.)

It's not the stuff of Dr. Spock.

But I'm not apologetic. When one mother gave her a plastic kitchen setup, I told another that Suki only played with it for five minutes, mostly with the battery-operated faucet. She admonished me, "Oh no, you have to pretend you have company and sit down for tea time." I fired back, "Forget it." Bag the kitchen, let's shoot hoops, where's Big Wheel? Yeah you're right, her bangs are too long, she doesn't know Barney from Barbie. But one thing she does know — this is better than Fuyang, where she was born.

Am I scared? I was at first, getting her — I feared I was going to China and returning with a She-Devil. Now — losing her. I'm afraid I'll slip up. Forget her typhoid shot. Leave her in J.C. Penney's. In the truck she chirps the alphabet, hits the wipers, unravels a cassette, yanks the steering wheel, points to every dog, "Doggie!" (Yes, I know, Suki. China has no dogs.) I'm afraid I can't lean across the seat to retrieve her barrette and keep us on the road, nine hundred times in a row. I'm never sure when I'm between the lines. And I'm afraid I'm not enough for her. I'm not Mama. My repeating to her that I'm both pa and ma has lost its oomph. How many women greet her for the first time and Suki dashes, arms windmilling, across the room? I shudder to think that quicker than she can say, *xie xie*, she'd be sweatless, ears scrubbed, hair pinned up, and in pink.

I'm afraid of being alone. That's new for me. When she's gone I see Suki's spoon, her dog-eared Mao book, the lost birdcaller under her bed, the red Z she made on my khakis with marker, her yellow frog in the tub. I get a flash: if she were gone? What if? My blood stops — suddenly I can't believe I'm this close to devastation.

How's the old ex-champ doing? In the grocery store, when I'm not looking, she snatches something off the shelf — *matzo* balls, rubber gloves, hemorrhoid cream, anything, and slips it into my basket. Two aisles later I discover it and hold it up like a dead fish, and she hurls her arms up. We howl, I'm a kid.

You can feel the eyes of other shoppers, mothers, peering eyes, envious eyes. "God, you are lucky." How many times have I heard that? In China it was, "Oh, she is a lucky girl." But little do they know. In my home study my social worker said, "Man, this guy did his homework!" And in Hangzhou, Hua Jun was always the last to go in from the courtyard — she knew something was over those walls.

We knew what we were doing. It's not luck.

Do I miss the days of sushi and Schubert? Do I resent the fact that every single night at nine for how many more years you can find me holding her hand, whispering, waiting for her sleepy, deep breaths?

The other night I left her for the very first time, after three months. A friend was to watch her while I went out, one simple cherished hour. I found her in the kitchen, singing away and scraping dishes (unassigned), and told her I was going swimming. She froze in the middle of the kitchen and wailed.

I slipped away and did my swim, sort of. In the middle of the second lap, I drifted to a stop. When I came home and opened the door, she jetted across the room into my arms. I hugged her as if it had been a lifetime, as if we had been an ocean apart. As if both our orphanages sprang up at our feet. I squeezed her as if my life depended on it.

Words Fail

Margaret Lawson

ON APRIL 12, 2000, we learned we were about to become parents to a six-month-old girl named Chun Fang. We named her Sophie and two months later we were en route to Hunan province to meet her. Sophie was a happy, active baby, and so it wasn't until months later that I realized she was also quiet. She just didn't seem to babble as you would expect a baby to babble. I began to worry.

I knew that speech and language delays were not uncommon among girls adopted from China. We had heard all about that back when we started considering and researching adoption from China. We had met adoptive parents who mentioned that their daughters were participating in speech therapy. I couldn't help but think about my own experience as a young child taking part in therapy sessions with Miss Lewis — whose name I couldn't pronounce correctly. As a pediatrician, I also couldn't help but think of the many families I had met over the years whose children needed some help to say what they meant.

Like most prospective parents, during the months that we waited for our referral I filled the time by reading and talking to people about issues our daughter might face. Some researchers hypothesized that the risk of language delay in children adopted internationally was related to the age of adoption. In contrast to what many people might expect, younger children appear to be at greater risk. Those adopted around the time of normal language acquisition — at six to twelve months — seem to be at higher risk than those who have already acquired some basic language in their mother tongue — more than twelve months. We had requested that our child be as young as possible and so I tried to prepare myself mentally for language delays. Still, I had no idea how those problems would feel when I faced them.

Once we brought Sophie home, she seemed to develop normally. My heart melted when, at eleven months, she said her first word: "Mama." By fifteen months, she could say five words and appeared to understand everything we said to her. In addition, our caregiver had been speaking French to Sophie from the time she was ten months, and Sophie seemed to understand that, too. For a while we wondered whether we had escaped the language problems so many parents and children faced. We had not.

In the fifteen years that I have been a pediatrician, I've become familiar with the milestones in language development. Knowing as I do what is normal and what is not, you would think I would know what to do with my own child. Unfortunately, it wasn't that easy. Like other parents of children adopted internationally, I had my share of comments from well-meaning but ill-informed bystanders. "Does she speak Chinese?" they'd ask when Sophie was only eight months old, an age when few babies speak any real language at all. "How long will it be before she can learn

English?" others wondered when Sophie was sixteen months old and had been home for eight months. Friends and relatives tried to reassure us: "It's the third language (French) that is slowing her down," or "You can't count the first eight months because she wasn't hearing English then." We discovered firsthand how easy and natural it was for us and others to make excuses when our child wasn't talking. To add to this, many parents are reluctant to admit that there are delays because we so want to prove to the outside world that our kids are normal. We want to defy naysayers who warned us about the risks of adopting a child from "over there."

I felt an extra burden because, as a pediatrician, it was especially hard for me to acknowledge that our child had a language delay and that I didn't know what to do to address it. Feeling helpless, I turned to other adoptive parents. At their advice, we took Sophie to one of the drop-in free consultative services offered in our area. After ten minutes of "talking with Sophie," who was by then eighteen months old, the speech pathologist agreed that she had significant expressive language delay that could not be explained by her first eight months in China or the fact that she was hearing English and French at home. Sophie was referred to the speech pathology department at our local children's hospital and we began the long wait for services.

Several months later, we were invited to an information session where speech experts explained to a room full of parents that isolated expressive language delay is common among otherwise normal children. We were also told that half these children will learn to speak on their own without any therapy. The problem, of course, is that there is no way to predict which children will or won't recover without intervention.

During the wait for therapy, the hospital offered some strategies we could use at home to help Sophie. Although Sophie clearly understood us when we told her to "go to your room and get your red running shoes and bring them to the front hall," the language structure was clearly too complicated for her to break down and play back with words she could use. Knowing this, we simplified our speech and began to say things like "Sophie, get red shoes." We felt a little stupid the first few times we gave instructions such as, "Eat cereal now," or "Wear coat, cold outside." But as Sophie began to understand us, we realized that speaking "stupid" was the smartest thing we could have done.

About six months passed before Sophie was called in for a detailed language assessment. By then she used thirty-five words, including counting to five and the nickname she had given herself, Yo-Yo, which was a huge improvement from the two words she used at eighteen months. But she still couldn't put the words together, and she continued to grunt and gesture to convey what she wanted. Because of this, the specialists decided to enroll Sophie in the Hanen program for children with isolated expressive language delay.

At first we were skeptical, especially my husband, and we wondered why other children had no problem learning to talk when their parents spoke in full sentences. Why do we have to dumb it down for our daughter? But after the first few classes, we realized that the program wasn't for Sophie, it was for us. The classes taught us as parents how to talk with our toddler in a way that would promote language development. It also became clear that most parents in our class were just as embarrassed and just as convinced as we were that they didn't need to be there. Emanating from us all was a feeling of denial and guilt. My husband and I realized that we needed to swallow our pride and focus on Sophie's needs. Each week we returned and learned more about how to talk with our daughter. After eight weeks we had a post-program assessment. Sophie had gone from 35 words to more than 350 English words plus about 50 French ones. She was putting two to four words together into sentences. She was still hard to understand — but then many two-year-olds are.

Even after the sessions we continued to use the Hanen principles in talking to Sophie and marveled at how she progressed in English and French. Soon Mandarin words and songs became part of her repertoire, too. She passed her annual assessments with flying colors and was discharged from the program the summer before her fourth birthday.

Today we wonder whether Sophie would have recovered without the Hanen program. We think she possibly would have, but probably not at such a rapid pace. Would a slower recovery have frustrated Sophie and us, and perhaps sparked behavioral problems? Fortunately, we'll never know.

What we do know is that just after Sophie's third birthday, friends from England came to visit along with their daughter. They had never met Sophie and after a few hours, we watched as Sophie connected with them. She talked nonstop to them and their daughter about a huge range of topics from the park up the street where she likes the swing, to what it's like to live in England. Just before leaving, they turned to us and said, "Sophie is so verbal." My husband and I looked at each other without saying a word and smiled.

At Home in a Small Town

Heidi Hatch

BROCKVILLE SITS ON THE BANKS of the St. Lawrence River in Eastern Ontario. Across the river, you can see upstate New York and on the other side of town, you'll find miles and miles of cedar bush and rocky Canadian Shield. It's the kind of place where most people consider themselves Brockvillians only after they've been here for several generations.

Although we work and go to school in Brockville, our home is in the country, with the cows and rabbits, a commuter-free drive away. The air is good and the stars after dark are fabulous. It's to this peaceful place that Bob and I brought our daughters home from China in 2000 and 2004.

Adopting from China was a natural choice for us. I had been a China fan for years and had always longed to travel there. But before we went to Asia to meet our first daughter, Chloe, we wondered how a transracially adopted child would fit in here in a mostly white town. Would she feel as though she belonged in a place where Chinatown consisted mostly of a few restaurants scattered along the main street?

We were confident that special groups and events for families adopting from China would help us expose our daughter to Chinese culture from time to time. But the nature of small-town life and the possibility of day-to-day issues for a Chinese child gave us pause. We wondered about racism. We also worried that our daughter would have very little chance to stay in touch with the culture of her birthplace. I'm happy to say that the past few years have proven us wrong.

Before we adopted, I was partly reassured and partly concerned by what a colleague had told me. Sunita was a bubbly young woman whose family had emigrated from India and who had just returned home from university. Raised in Brockville, she seemed like a good candidate to ask about life in a small town for someone visibly different. I asked whether she had faced discrimination growing up. After some thought, she said she'd had a happy childhood, blending in with her peers and enjoying her innocence. Laughing, she talked about one situation that made her feel different. "I got sick of always having to play the role of Uhura when we played *Star Trek* at school."

But she said that fitting in became more complicated when she went away to university in a large city. There, not only did she feel less than welcomed by her white classmates, but she was also unable to really connect with other South Asian students. She thought that she felt different from them because as a child she hadn't socialized with many South Asians apart from her immediate family. The cultural differences presented a barrier, and for the first time in her life, Sunita questioned who she was, and where she belonged.

I kept this in mind as we settled into a new life with Chloe in late autumn 2000. I took a year off work and everywhere I went, Chloe went with me. She became a regular at the Y drop-in playgroup, local stores and cafés, restaurants and parks. If our family stood out, it was rarely pointed out to us. We had occasional comments — "Is she adopted?" and "Oh, she's so cute" — but nothing negative. Chloe became recognized around town and so did I, as Chloe's mom.

When I returned to work, Chloe usually went to daycare. One afternoon when the babysitter was sick, I took the day off and went with Chloe to the Y for a romp in the big gym. My attention was drawn to two Chinese women chatting by the sandbox. They noticed us, too, and I couldn't help but wonder what they thought of me and my daughter. I noticed that they had young children and was eager to meet them. Despite a feeling that they were talking about me, I smiled and said hello. Both women broke out in huge smiles. In heavily accented English one of them asked about Chloe. Where is she from? Was she my daughter? What was her Chinese name? I told them Chloe was named Ling Ran by the director of her orphanage. "Ran" means correct and "Ling" has several meanings, although the one we like is ice. Correct Ice seems to suit a December baby.

Both women chatted to Chloe in Chinese and called her Ling Ran. I love Chloe's Chinese name and enjoyed hearing them use it.

Sophia Chen and Yang Hong had both moved to town from China within the previous five years. They had met here in Brockville and become good friends. That day, we talked about the things mothers talk about to each other. When I mentioned why I was off work, Sophia offered to babysit if I ever got stuck for child care again. I thanked her and held on to the thought.

A week or so later, the babysitter called to say she couldn't take Chloe. I wasn't sure that Sophia really had meant her offer but I remembered her name and called. To my relief, Sophia was delighted to take my preschooler for a day.

The trial day was a success. When I came to pick up Chloe, soft Chinese music played in the background. There was not a television in sight. Chloe eagerly showed me a pile of wet, gluey paper. "Look Mama, look what we did today." Her name was written in Chinese characters. I stood in the doorway and felt the prick of tears behind my eyes. Chloe was in the middle of a Chinese family, surrounded by Chinese music and the smell of deliciously spiced food. I felt the huge loss of her family in China.

Chloe and Yun Zhe, Sophia's daughter, had hit it off immediately. It was obvious that Sophia was a wonderful mother and that she had provided excellent care. Her parenting was easygoing; she had done crafts with the children, and was by no means a heavy disciplinarian. Sophia reported that Chloe loved glue, and had dumplings for lunch. Sophia asked me whether it was okay to call Chloe "Ling Ran." I thought it was fantastic.

Thrilled by how the day had gone, Bob and I decided we would ask Sophia whether she could take Chloe on a regular basis. After the first few days with Sophia, Chloe cried when I left her. I guessed that she was objecting to the transition largely because Sophia spoke to her in Mandarin. I wondered if we were doing the right thing. After some consideration, we decided that a Chinese babysitter was the best thing for Chloe even if she didn't think so at first.

We believe now that it was the best choice. Sophia spoke Mandarin with Chloe from the beginning and, even though Chloe spoke only a little, it was apparent after a few months that she understood a lot. One day at pick-up time, we sat at the bottom of Sophia's stairs chatting about the day and what the children had done. Chloe showed Sophia little bits of paper she had taped to her nails, a kind of do-it-yourself manicure. Yun Zhe giggled;

they looked silly on Chloe's little fingers. With a shrug and a smile, Chloe asked Sophia what she should do with them. Sophia answered her in a Chinese sentence of at least twenty-five words. Chloe paused, then said, "Okay then," and ran to the garbage can. Sophia had told her that if she didn't want the papers she should throw them away before she left.

I was astounded and proud that Chloe could understand. Even though she had heard Chinese for the first nine months of her life, Chloe had shown no recognition of her native tongue when she was reintroduced to it.

As well as slowly learning Mandarin, Chloe was benefiting from her exposure to daily life with a Chinese family. Sophia and her husband Bill often had family and friends as guests. Chloe was comfortable being picked up, poked, and prodded by an aged auntie, happy to go off to play with various cousins, and she didn't seem lost or out of place at large gatherings. She was often surrounded by people speaking Chinese and she was at ease with it.

Over the next eighteen months, we started our second adoption and Sophia became pregnant. She and her family returned to China to visit. She talked to many people in her hometown in Hunan about Chloe and the other little girls she had met from China. She was happy to tell her friends in Hunan that the adoptees she had met were well cared for. She said that most people at home did not know about international adoption.

Sophia gave birth to her second daughter in December 2003, and we adopted Meiling shortly after in January 2004. When Sophia took two months off work, her friend Yang Hong offered to babysit Chloe. Luckily, her son Kevin is the same age as Chloe and we engineered it so that they would be in the same class. They were the only Chinese children in kindergarten.

Kevin began school without a word of English. A painfully shy boy, Kevin clung to Chloe at school. He was usually in the playground before the morning bell rang, standing rigid, hands stuck to his sides. Not so shy at home or with other Chinese families, he likes to scare Chloe by shoving Goosebumps books into her face, making her look at pictures of monsters. It's easy to pick out my daughter and her best friend in the annual class photograph, their faces the image of the change happening in communities across Canada.

We were delighted with the care Yang Hong provided. After a few days with Yang Hong, Chloe proudly showed me a little homemade dictionary with four pages filled out. Yang Hong stood back a few paces, smiling. On each line Yang had written a word in English, then the Chinese character, then the English spelling of the Chinese word. Finally, on each line she had written a phonetic way to pronounce the word — presumably to help me.

I attempted to read the words, causing Chloe and Kevin to giggle behind their hands. Chloe acted the teacher — a role she loves — grabbing the book and asking, "Mummy, do you know how to say hello to a man you would meet on the street"?

"*Ni hao*," I said, knowing that Chloe is dying to correct me.

"No, it's *Shu shu hao* if the man is older than you and more important," she told me, jumping up and down. "And it's *Aiyi hao* for a woman." Yang Hong said that Chloe had good pronunciation and got the tones just right.

Chloe had another announcement. "I'm not going to suck my thumb in China. Only in the hotel room." I agreed that was a good idea. "In China it's dirty to suck your thumb," she informed me. I remembered this all too clearly from our trip in 2000. It was common for women to reach over and pull her thumb out of her mouth, undeterred by the baby's frantic wails. We, her parents, were given severe finger wags for allowing such unhygienic behavior.

Yang Hong's cultural coaching paid off well. When we went

Chloe

Meiling

to China to adopt Meiling, Chloe came with us and seemed so at ease, comfortable with the sometimes intrusive (by Canadian standards) locals who talked to her and touched her.

Sophia and I enjoyed the perfect timing of our maternity leaves, getting together regularly to let the four girls play. She became a good friend, so much more than just Chloe's babysitter. We talked for hours about life in China and life in Canada. I introduced her to pub food, walks in the woods, and consignment clothing shops. She introduced me to spicy Hunan dishes, Chinese New Year, and a set of new friends otherwise unavailable to our family.

As our children played together, we talked about our relationships with our families, our views on childrearing, governments, laws, and lifestyles. She has given me valuable insight into the issues our children's birth families would have faced in China. We have talked at length about the life of rural and urban Chinese, rich and poor. As the mother of two girls, she has helped me to understand the complex feelings many Chinese people have toward girl children, and their role in families.

One day Sophia and I were shopping together. While she shopped for food, I took all four children with me — two in the cart and two scampering alongside. I couldn't help but smile at the curious looks we got from an Asian woman who watched. I wondered what she was thinking. Too many children? Too noisy? Or are they really all mine? Sometimes people think all four are Sophia's and I am the nanny. The children don't look anything like each other, but most people don't notice that.

In the past few years it has become apparent that we were mistaken to think that our town lacked cultural diversity. Since we got to know Sophia's family we have met many other Chinese families and we've been welcomed into the Chinese community with open arms. For years, we've attended Lunar New Year celebrations, hosted by the local Chinese Cultural Association. We have been invited to barbecues and birthday parties where my husband and I are the only non-Chinese. Everyone is friendly and interested in our children. We're grateful to our new friends for the way they have accepted us into their lives.

Our experience with adoption in a small town has been as positive as we could have hoped for. We feel that Chloe and Meiling are comfortable and at home with many kinds of families — their school friends' families, who are "typical" Canadian birth families mostly of European descent, families with adopted children from China, and Chinese families. So far, we have experienced no racism, discrimination, or hostility, just the mild curiosity of people who are mostly well-wishers.

A few summers ago we hosted a party, inviting friends with children from China and our Chinese friends. One of the guests marveled at the group playing badminton, splashing in the wading pool, and feeding the horses. "How did you manage it?" She is a longtime international adoption expert and an advocate of cross-cultural mixing. But even in her urban, multiracial neighborhood she had not been able to form solid, real friendships with local Chinese families. She was in awe of what we had, way out in the country.

I admit I sat back that warm day and felt satisfied with the way things had worked out. It was good to see Chloe and Meiling running and splashing, playing happily with this unique blend of friends.

We know that one day our children may not be interested in "Chinese things"; they may reject their roots and history as they try to blend in with their peers. But they will have had a taste of China, and the choice will be theirs.

Bullets on the Bund:
An Excerpt

Steve Whan

MY WIFE AND I HAVE ADOPTED two girls from China. In January 1999, we were doing the paperwork to adopt our second daughter. I was at the computer filling out some forms, when it hit me. I read the Hardy Boys when I was young and my sisters read Nancy Drew. Where were the mystery stories for Asian kids, especially all of the girls adopted from China?

Within a couple of days, I had roughed out the concept of a heroine who was adopted from China, lived in Vancouver, and solved mysteries with the help of dreams about Shanghai in the 1930s. I used the English translation of my first daughter's Chinese name for the main character: Autumn Jade.

I had written technical articles, but I had never felt a burning desire to write a young adult novel. The writing went so well that I sent a publisher a query letter. Less than two weeks later I had a reply requesting my manuscript . . . which wasn't finished, of course, because I hadn't expected to get a reply so quickly.

We polished the manuscript and sent it off again, only to wait a year for a rejection letter. But I felt so strongly about having this book for my daughters to read that I formed my own publishing company.

There are now four books in the Autumn Jade Mystery series in print with more than 4,000 copies sold all over the world. This was not something I had ever planned to do, but our two daughters have been such a powerful influence on my life that the writing seemed like a natural step. It's a gift I can give back to them.

I've read this excerpt many times to my daughters. It wasn't easy the first time, but it served its original purpose of generating discussion on the issues surrounding their abandonment.

Chapter One, *Bullets on the Bund*

The early morning mist rolled gently off the Whangpoo River and up onto The Bund, the main street of Shanghai's International Settlement. Ming found it amazing that clean, white mist could come off a river that was so yellow and filthy. People said that if you watched long enough, you would eventually see a body floating by.

There was a constant, bewildering sound of music in the air: the carrier coolies chanting to lighten their heavy loads and regulate their breathing, the subdued singing of men and women poling their sampans across the river. But Ming had no song in her heart today.

Liang Ming had come to Shanghai with several other women from her village. They had bananas, small and green, and ripe pomelos to sell at the market. Ming had another reason to be in the city. She carried a tiny, hidden bundle that she held close to her breast. The baby girl was only a day old. Ming hadn't thought she could feel so much love for such a little creature. Yet she had fed the infant with the milk of her body, and she felt the bond strengthen with every beat of her daughter's heart.

She could still remember the marriage ceremony ten months earlier. The Chen clan had consulted fortune-tellers for months in order to find a bride who would produce a boy for their eldest son. She had been the girl they had chosen. She had never been so happy as she was on her wedding day.

The marriage feast had been lavish and all the customs had been followed. She had been fetched from her parent's home, dressed in the finest red-and-gold cloth, her hair entwined with pearls and jade, bracelets on her arms and rings on each tiny finger. There were kowtows made to the images of the ancestors and five pigs were killed for the banquet. The guests ate glutinous rice cakes in abundance and the rice wine flowed. Everyone seemed to be already celebrating the birth of a new baby boy.

Ming's new husband and his family were most gentle with the new bride. The birth of a baby boy was the highest priority and she was told not to go into the fields or to labor too hard.

Soon after the marriage, the pulse of a new life was beating through Ming's veins. It was the time for praying. All the women of the village lit candles and incense and on bent knees chanted prayers to Guan Yin, Goddess of Compassion, for the blessing of a son. The months passed quickly and soon it was time for the birth.

With her husband at her side and family members waiting nearby, the birth of the new baby went smoothly. Ming was unprepared for the elation she felt, the exhilaration of having carried a perfectly beautiful and healthy child to term. Even the dreary hut, the cold bed, and the impersonal midwife couldn't dim her happiness. Ming looked closely at the new baby, tracing the tiny ears, delicate nose, and smiling mouth with her finger. She had created a child, a real child. Life was beginning for a new person, separate and marvelous.

Perhaps the fortune had been poorly told, or perhaps she had encountered a peach ghost during her pregnancy. The nightmare began when her husband's mother entered the room and saw the naked child.

"How could you do this to us! It is a girl baby. We have no need for girls, she will have to be killed," her husband's Honorable Mother had shouted at her.

Her husband's younger brother threatened to beat the luckless soothsayer and also to beat Ming.

Old Auntie said, "Send Liang Ming back to her own family, she has brought us much disgrace."

Other Chen family clan members spoke of revenge as well. Through it all, her husband refused to look at his wife or the infant.

Then, quietly, the family resolved the problem between themselves.

"We will say that the baby disappeared during the night, taken away by the same ghosts who entered Ming and robbed her of the boy that was hers by right." Everyone agreed.

Ming was told to leave for Shanghai in the early hours of the morning with the other family members who were going to sell their fruit. She was to abandon the baby girl somewhere along the way. Death would be swift for a child left out in the open. With the whole family against her and with her husband refusing to even look at her, Ming had no choice but to agree.

Before Ming had traveled very far though, she had changed her mind. She had decided to disobey the family and when the time came, she only pretended to leave her baby in a farmer's rice field. Frightened and desperate, she was now in the city with her daughter still tucked away under her clothing, hidden from the others. She had resolved to abandon her baby somewhere public enough that she would be quickly found, but private enough that no one would see Ming do it. Now that Ming was in Shanghai, she realized it might not be so easy.

Ming knew that only a foreigner or wealthy Chinese might save her child. But the British Consulate had guards at the gate and the foreign hotels were too crowded. She was scared sick. Her heart was beating too fast and there was a huge knot in her belly. She was worried now that her trembling might wake the child and then she would be caught.

There were tales about a place with a 'baby-drawer,' a small wooden panel in a high brick wall where the child could be left. Chinese *amahs* under the supervision of Roman Catholic nuns raised the children. Ming didn't know where this building was and she didn't have the time to look for it.

Ahead of her, Ming could see a tall building with an enormous clock on the tower. The sign said Customs House and there were foreigners of all kinds in sight. Large packing crates and stacks of burlap-wrapped bundles provided cover, yet would soon be moved to their exotic destinations. This looked like it might be the place. It had to be the place. They were almost at the market and she was running out of time.

"I have to stop for a moment," Ming said to the others. "I will catch up."

"Are you okay?" asked her sister-in-law Chen Hua. "I can wait for you."

"No, keep on going, I will catch up shortly," Ming said, pointing at her bladder. Everyone nodded and they continued on without her.

Safely secluded, Ming whispered quietly to herself, "Ancestors, please give me strength. Mama's taking you out now, my precious child. Shh, shh, shh, don't cry. Don't cry now. I'm laying you softly on the ground where you will be found. Please don't hate me for this, I was given no choice."

Ming removed a pendant from around her neck. The teardrop-shaped piece of rare, purple jade had an intricate carving of an Imperial dragon on one side.

"This jade pendant comes from my mother and her mother before her. I place it around your neck hoping it brings you a happier life than mine."

Ming's bitter tears splashed onto her daughter's rosy cheek.

"*Zaijian*, my little one. Your mama will always love you, no matter where you are. Together we were whole, now I will be an empty shell. I promise that not a day will go by that I won't think about the daughter I had to give away."

It was too late to change her mind, she could hear footsteps approaching. Ming wiped her eyes and took several deep, sobbing breaths. Then she quickly turned and hurried to catch up with the others.

Why Not an Egg?

Shelley Page

THREE DAYS AFTER she was placed in my arms, I bound my new daughter to my chest and we took our first tentative steps alone into the twisting streets of Changsha. I was scared, to tell the truth. I didn't know a word of Mandarin and was worried we might get lost in the alleys and dead ends surrounding our hotel. That would be no way to win the confidence of my eight-month-old daughter. But I needed to escape our cramped, diaper-strewn hotel room and a jet-lagged husband. It was cold and windy, but I positioned Cleo outward, thinking she'd want to see the world. I forgot the world could see her, or us. We were still a strange sight in 1999, a tall, freckled, white woman packing a tiny Chinese girl with rose-petal lips.

People followed as we walked. Crowds formed when we stopped, encircling us. Out of nowhere, ancient, stooped Chinese women appeared and started tugging and fussing with my child's clothing. Gnarled fingers adjusted her scarf so it covered more of her face, and then sampled her snowsuit fabric to make sure it was thick enough. I'd been warned that all over China packs of grannies — the clothing police — seemed to roam the streets looking for inept Westerners who hadn't dressed their Chinese babies warmly enough. These clucking women bombarded me with questions.

"I'm sorry. I don't speak Chinese," I muttered. They kept at me, but louder. With one hand firmly on my baby, I yanked on a string around my neck and pulled out a card that explained our situation in neat Chinese characters.

"I am Canadian. This is my new daughter. She is an orphan. She will live in Canada with us. We will always take care of her. Thank you."

The women leaned in and deciphered the words, looked at me and my daughter with a mix of curiosity and bewilderment, then spoke to each other in conspiratorial tones. I nodded politely and then fled with Cleo.

I hated how that exchange made me feel.

In just a few short days, my daughter had already been separated from her culture and her past because her new mother could not communicate with her people. I felt like I was letting her down.

Before my husband and I adopted our first daughter, our social worker loaded us up with articles on the difficulties of transracial adoption and research papers on the psychological health of international adoptees. We read about the experience of the thousands of Korean children adopted by North Americans starting in the early 1950s. Often, these were not success stories. Many adult Korean adoptees were unhappy and bitter. They grew up isolated from each other and from Korean-Americans in general. These adult adoptees knew nothing of their language or culture. Depression was common. So was anger. Their identity questions were profound: were they white or Korean? Some described themselves as bananas: yellow on the outside, white on the inside.

We assured our social worker — and the Chinese government when we wrote asking permission to adopt — that we would do all in our power to learn from the experience of the Korean adoptions of an earlier era. Our girls would be raised in a celebration of their culture. We would acknowledge the Lunar New Year with dumplings and dragons and lanterns. We would enroll our daughters in Chinese dance classes and in Mandarin lessons on Saturday mornings. We would redecorate our homes in Chinese red with gold-trimmed lanterns. We would learn to eat Chinese food with chopsticks. We wouldn't let our daughters forget the country from which we had taken them, despite the fact most of us were armchair experts without firsthand knowledge of China.

My husband and I returned home with Cleo and bought *Big Bird Goes to China* translated into Chinese, read her *Mulan* at bedtime, and found a Mandarin-speaking babysitter to visit a few times a week. As Bin taught Cleo Chinese songs and basic Chinese words, I remained in a nearby room, folding laundry or making baby food. I'd eavesdrop but not participate. This seemed wrong to me, too. Cleo and I should be in this together.

The other students in the classroom, inside a red brick building just off Ottawa's scrawny Chinatown, were drawn largely from the industries that dominate the city. There were Foreign Service workers heading to postings in China and computer whizzes planning to set up Chinese cell phone networks in Inner Mongolia. There were also Cantonese-speaking immigrants who realized that Mandarin offered a brighter future. Besides me, there was one other mother of an adopted Chinese girl. She stayed for only six weeks.

Many days I wanted to quit, too. I calculated I had nine months to learn as much of the language as possible before heading to China to adopt our second daughter. I wasn't sure what I could learn in that time, but I was determined to make the grandmothers understand why so many of China's baby girls had to fly to the other side of the world to find a family.

I had read that it takes four times as long to learn Mandarin as it does to learn Spanish or French. That unsettled me. I had studied French most of my life, including stints in Nice and Chicoutimi, and never achieved fluency. What made me think I would have any greater success at Mandarin, with its characters and tones so different from Western languages?

I dutifully sat in the class and repeated the four tones, one going up, another down, one flat, and the last with a dip in the middle that sounds like a moan. I learned how the word *"mao"* could have many different meanings depending on pronunciation and context. With the wrong slip of the tongue over the palette, what I meant to be cat could become hat, or even the former leader of the Communist Party.

My Chinese professor was smart and realized the frustration level was high. She had us speaking short sentences by the second week. Instead of toiling exclusively over tones, I learned to say *"Wo shi Jianada xuesheng,"* or "I am a Canadian student," and other phrases. At night I scrawled Chinese characters over and over in my notebook until I had them memorized and then I wrote them clearly on flashcards. The months passed and the stack grew by my bed, which is where I did most of my studying after Cleo fell asleep.

Students dropped out because of time commitments or frustration. I couldn't quit, even when I wanted to. I guess I was too committed, or too stubborn. Besides, I had grandmothers to meet. So I counted down the days. By early April, nine months after I began and two weeks before I was to leave for China, I had memorized 500 characters and dozens of sentences. My teacher assured me that was enough to get by. I was excited and nervous to test-drive a language that so far I'd only taken for a spin around the classroom. Cleo, then four, and I would once again stroll the streets of China, and this time, we would be able to explain ourselves.

It didn't happen. Unfortunately, our second trip to adopt was rife with setbacks. A mysterious respiratory illness called SARS seized China, and the Canadian government warned adoptive parents not to take small children or elderly people when we went to get our babies. My mom had been planning to come along with Cleo, but we decided to make the trip without them. My elder daughter would not get to see me answer those Chinese grandmothers with the responses I'd carefully practiced. I'd already learned the Chinese words for adoption and orphanage — which weren't in the textbooks. Now I had to memorize quarantine, SARS, and face mask.

There was a persistent rumor that North Americans had brought SARS to China. This meant few crowds gathered around us as we walked the almost-deserted streets with our second daughter, Scarlet, tied to my chest. Instead of facing her outward, we kept her turned inward, away from the hot, potentially lethal breath of strangers. There weren't any grandmothers on the streets and most civilians covered their faces when they saw us coming. Mostly it was the vendors in the Silk Alley who peppered us with questions. "Lady, Lady, would you like to buy a nice purse?" "Lady, Lady, you want to buy socks?" As we passed I could make out some of their conversations about us, the *"wai guo ren"* or foreigners. I'd turn and smile and speak a few words in Mandarin. Almost all my purchases were greatly discounted: a reward for my efforts.

On that trip, I ordered food, bought silk ties and chopsticks, and talked to Scarlet's nannies at her orphanage, gleaning important information about her personality, likes, and dislikes. At night, while Scarlet slept, I did my homework in our hotel room. This experience was inspiring. It seemed reasonable that if our kids might end up as bananas, I could be an egg, with a white shell and a beautiful yolk in the middle.

It was the middle of July and Cleo sat in a classroom filled with other Chinese students. All were writing row upon row of characters. It was her third week of Mandarin immersion summer school, part of the Ottawa school board's international language program. There were hundreds of children enrolled. All had Chinese parents except for one other student. At four, Cleo was still too young to really notice racial differences, so to her I was just like any other mom there. Tell that to the other parents; I confused them.

With fourteen-month-old Scarlet on my hip, I once again fielded questions from the many Chinese immigrants who wanted their children to hold on to their mother tongue. While they thought Mandarin was important for their children, they were shocked that I would bother in a land where English was so dominant. They were equally shocked that I had learned Chinese, and it was amazing to see their faces light up as I stumbled along, struggling to make myself understood.

I learned that summer a lesson I will never forget: what it means for immigrants to find someone who can speak to them in their own language, someone who can welcome them and be friends with them in their new country. The moms and dads I met in the corridor outside Cleo's classroom would show up some days with their elderly parents walking behind them. Usually these seniors were visiting for several months to help with the babysitting, and sometimes they too were immigrants. They never spoke a word of English and few had ever spoken to a "genuine" Canadian; that is, someone white and English-speaking. Their adult children would nudge them toward me and encourage them to ask simple questions in Mandarin about the weather, Ottawa, or my children.

These awkward exchanges would mark the first time many of them had ever had a conversation with a Canadian, even if it was in Mandarin. But as much as my Mandarin amused and impressed them, it was Cleo and Scarlet whom they wanted to hear speak their language. They would prod and cajole Cleo into muttering "*Ni hao*," or "*Wo jiao Cleo*." From what I could figure out, they firmly believed that without the ability to speak their language, my girls were not authentically Chinese. Language was everything. These new friends wanted to help. They invited my family to their apartments and fed us eight-course dinners while we sat on plastic crates. My daughters soon had honorary Chinese grandparents all over the city.

Courtesy Glen McGregor

After that experience, I went out of my way to speak to new immigrants I saw struggling through daily life, at grocery store checkouts and in doctors' offices. Once, a cashier was making fun of a Chinese woman who didn't have enough cash to pay for the sixteen pineapples she had just bought. The cashier tried to draw me in on the laugh, but instead I turned and began chatting with the woman, offering her the few extra quarters she needed. Her face brightened, as others before had. It was like giving an unexpected gift that said their language and culture was valued. And if they felt that way, what about my girls? Children are observant. Every one of these encounters has told my children that their language, culture, and people matter to me, and my husband, who had also begun to learn the language. But just as we began to immerse ourselves further, planning a trip to live in Beijing to study the language, friends told us that they were finding it more difficult to make a cultural connection. Their kids didn't want to learn Mandarin. Some didn't even like talking about China — the topic was greeted with an indifferent shrug. Other parents told us that they were worried if they pushed too hard, their kids would turn away completely. We couldn't help but wonder if they might be right. How long would it be before our daughters rebelled against our efforts?

When Scarlet was two and Cleo was five, I was invited to take part in a panel discussion for transracial adoptive families on how to bring our children's culture into their lives. It was a bitterly cold Ottawa day and the event was in a cavernous room adjacent to a hockey arena. There was no heat. The venue was packed with families, parents of Chinese, Vietnamese, African-American, and African-Canadian children, among many other backgrounds. The father of an adopted African-Canadian child spoke first, saying that he didn't think it all that necessary to pay attention to what he called "black culture" and that his son was doing just fine without any adult black role models. It was impossible not to notice nods of approval from the mostly white crowd.

Then an adult aboriginal adoptee told a harrowing story of being adopted in the 1970s by an abusive family. They ignored his heritage and treated him as though he was ignorant and stupid because he wasn't white. As a teenager, he turned to drugs and lived on the streets. His story was heartbreaking, and many in the audience cried. He'd spent years trying to figure out who he was after his adoptive parents had erased his past.

It was difficult to follow such a poignant and tragic story. I spoke about the young Chinese women we'd found to act as mentors for our girls so that white faces wouldn't always surround them, about how we'd had both girls in Mandarin instruction since they were toddlers, and about our Mandarin-speaking nanny. At Christmas, Easter, and Thanksgiving, we invited Chinese immigrants into our home and shared our turkey and other Canadian customs. In return, we accepted invitations to their homes. I told them about our upcoming trip to Beijing to study. Before I'd even finished speaking, some members of the audience heckled me.

"We're in Canada now!" one man shouted to loud applause.

"We're all Canadians," said another.

I was confused. Based on the discussion that followed, it was obvious that some, but not all, of the parents thought me foolish and my efforts extreme and unrealistic. I knew many in the audience were moved by the aboriginal adoptee's story, yet they seemed to think it was okay to take a Chinese baby away from her language and her culture. It was difficult for me to see the difference between the two situations.

I'm not saying everyone should learn their child's mother tongue, but I think children should be given a shot at learning the language, or be provided with mentors and experiences that reflect their heritages in a positive light.

None of the choices we make for our kids is easy. Between the carpooling, crazy schedules, and financial stress, it can all get too difficult. We end up choosing ballet over Saturday morning Mandarin classes, hamburgers over General Tso's chicken, soccer over Chinese dance, the babysitter next door instead of a Chinese-Canadian teenager a fifteen-minute drive away. None is a simple choice. But even if we don't have time to do it all, we don't have to toss everything out.

Some parents that stressful night told me that they'd rather their girls fit in than be different. But our girls are different. They always will be. Not just because of the color of their skin but because of the way our families were formed. But I hope the language lessons and cultural influences will make them confident in, even celebrate, their differences, instead of noticing only that they don't look like their classmates.

When Cleo volunteers to talk about her adoption anniversary in class, or when she quietly fills red envelopes with chocolate for her classmates on Lunar New Year, or when she proudly recites her Mandarin homework to anyone who will listen, it's because she likes who she is and wants to share it. She is fitting in because of who she is — the whole package — instead of fitting in by her difference. Or so I thought.

Cleo was seven when she told me she wanted to quit Mandarin.

Her reason was simple. It was too hard and it took up too much time. She'd been at it for four years and was now the only adopted Chinese child in her class at a private weekend language school. The other children either had Chinese parents or were Caucasians with ambitious parents who wanted them to learn Chinese.

I ignored Cleo the first time.

Then she asked me again. And again.

"If you want to quit, you can quit." As soon as the words were out of my mouth, I wanted to retract them.

Days went by. She didn't do her homework that week. She went to class ill-prepared and came home frustrated. She pleaded with me to allow her to drop the class, then and there, and not finish the semester. I lay awake at night worrying that this was not the right decision. I thought of those sad Korean adoptees who said they just wished their parents had pushed a little harder.

We went for bubble tea in Chinatown. I told her that, as her parents, we would sometimes make decisions for her that she might disagree with, and in this case, we thought her language was too important to give up on. And I also told her that quitting was too easy. I knew her well enough to know she liked challenges. Language was a challenge, her challenge. She nodded intently.

I don't think I'd ever explained so clearly the reasons she was learning the language. Afterward, she rededicated herself to her studies. She took her Mandarin homework to her after-school program, and loved to show her friends the meanings of the mysterious characters. And sometimes she used my words against me. We were invited to the Chinese Embassy for a cultural performance, but I didn't think she should miss gymnastics twice in a row.

"So you're saying you think gymnastics is more important then my culture?" she asked. Needless to say, she skipped gymnastics.

Some may think I am wrong for forcing her, but if I don't support her language and culture, who will? If I let her drop her language, what message does that send? That it's not worth the effort? One day she may quit, or she may enroll in a course in China and claim full ownership over the language she was born to. We can only guide her so far.

We were in the remote mountains of Yunnan in 2006 — our second trip as a family to China — standing before a ramshackle restaurant with much of the day's lunch pecking in the dirt around our feet. The cook asked us in Mandarin what we wanted. Cleo pointed at the bowls of green vegetables. "*Nage. He nage,*" she said shyly. That one. And that one. Then she pointed at the pecking bird and said "*jirou,*" or chicken. We would be having it fresh for lunch. The cook asked us where we were from. In a quiet but proud voice, Cleo explained: "*Women shi Jianadaren he wo cong Zhongguo lai.*"

"We are Canadian, and I come from China."

Out of the Mouths of Babies

Lilian Nattel

THIS IS MY FAMILY: we are white parents with Chinese kids, Jewish, vegetarian, artistic, academic, swimmers, skaters, and especially eaters. Most of our celebrations revolve around food. We value diversity. This is entirely Canadian. As the judges of the Seven Wonders of Canada said: being Canadian is all about compromise. My daughters' first names are Hebrew, their middle names Chinese. They are turning nine and six in the next couple of months. Last night, when I came in to kiss them goodnight, my older daughter was sitting at her table, writing a story and illustrating it, wanting to know about how to get it published. My little one was on her bed, playing with a chocolate cake factory that she made by assembling a miniature baby carriage full of pennies (the cakes), a pony corral, and a Playmobil shopping cart. They both take swimming lessons and skating lessons and neither of them takes either Hebrew or Chinese, though during the adoption process, I was sure that my children would become fluent in both. Instead, because my first child wanted me to take her skating, I enrolled in the adult class at our local arena, discovering that I love to skate. This is what I've learned as a parent: my children are reforming me more than I am forming them.

I expected something very different before traveling to China. It was my plan to be Super Adoptive Mom. Our house would be infused with Chinese culture as well as Jewish culture. Our children would learn Hebrew and Chinese. We would celebrate every holiday in the fullest, most traditional way. I agonized over what complications this would bring to them. I considered whether they would encounter prejudice in the Jewish community and whether I was burdening them with Hebrew first names. My husband and I debated over public school versus Jewish day school. We had no idea that being parents would overwhelm us with much more basic concerns, like enduring tantrums and studying the frequency, size, and texture of baby poop. It seemed in those early days like they would be babies forever. Their first conscious identity was of being vegetarian. As a preschooler, my older daughter liked to walk around the grocery store and look at the meat and fish. In a very loud, inquisitive voice she'd say, "Is that *meat*? Do people eat that? What is it?"

Photo courtesy Lilian Nattel

Life with kids is a day-in and day-out affair, all-absorbing at each stage. The major choice my husband and I made was to take advantage of our flexible work schedules to spend more time with the girls, and, especially before they started school, to minimize daycare. Beyond that, we have tended to take the path of least resistance, like putting our daughters in the public school and enrolling them in activities at the Boys and Girls club and the arena because they're all within walking distance. Now, all of a sudden, my older daughter, born in the year of the tiger (I can attest to the cuddliness and the claws), is going into grade 4. And my little snake baby, who wriggled out of her highchair and her stroller, is starting grade 1. She'll be at school all day. And I agreed to write about the multiple layers of their identities.

While we're all together in my room, I decide to have a conversation with them about it. My older daughter, the tiger, throws herself into life with zeal, but you can't get anything out of her about her personal opinions and feelings until she is ready to share it — usually in a single sentence once or twice a year. However, my little one is always happiest talking and thinking aloud. We're watching part of our endless supply of *Land Before Time* videos. (Spike, the dinosaur baby who always likes to eat, is adopted. My favorite episode is the one where he is trapped under the frozen lake and calls out "Mama," his first word, as she comes leaping through the ice to save him.) My tiger daughter and I are on the bed, and she's leaning against my knees. My soon-to-be six-year-old is sitting on the floor, playing with a dollhouse. I start by asking what she likes best about being a vegetarian. Her answer is "not eating meat." That's straightforward so far. The other questions I want to ask my daughters are more complex.

I've fielded a lot of calls from Jewish families referred to me by our adoption agency. They usually want to know if there's been any negative reaction in the Jewish community. I tell them honestly that I've never experienced any. But we've stopped going to synagogue for the most part. That had nothing to do with prejudice or my children being Chinese. One factor is that, as I've continued to change and grow, the services no longer fit with my own spirituality. The other factor was the exhausting logistics. Spending Saturday morning with my kids all dressed up and bored is not my idea of a socially or spiritually uplifting experience. Taking them to the library and then to the park or swimming pool wasn't particularly Jewish, but it was peaceful and sweet. As they got older, they began to play together. The first Saturday morning I slept in until ten, I ran downstairs to check whether my children were in one piece. *Shabbat* (Sabbath) morning is a time for me to catch up on my sleep, a time for my daughters to play together without competing for our attention, sneak snacks, paint, draw, set up a train made out of chairs in the living room. So we have become what I never expected to be: revolving-door Jews, into synagogue at Rosh Hashanah and out at Yom Kippur. Bagel and lox Jews. Minus the lox. Minus the bagels, too. Luckily for me, my husband is a really good vegetarian cook. Every Friday night we light candles, we have wine and say the blessing over it and the Sabbath *Kiddush*. We eat pasta, smoked tofu with horseradish and yogurt sauce, and vegetables in season. The girls have chocolate croissants. Then on Saturday afternoon, they get another treat of their choice, usually chips or an ice cream cone.

While my younger daughter (who loves pink) fixes her hair with assorted clips, I ask her what she likes best about being Jewish. She says, "Do people who have Christmas have *Shabbat*?" I tell her they don't. She adds, "That's what I like best, having a chocolate croissant on *Shabbat*."

When I ask her what she likes best about being Chinese, she says that Chinese people know what year it is — the year of the dragon, the pig, the rooster — so that if someone asks, you know.

But in circle time her daycare teacher asked her what year it is now because she's Chinese and she didn't know, so she hid behind her friends. My older daughter is growing out her bangs; hair hangs over her eyes. She shouts, "It's the year of the pig!" Her little sister answers, "Oh. Daddy was born in the year of the pig."

I ask her if she would like my husband and me to be Chinese, too. She says, "Yes." I ask her what she'd like about that, thinking she's going to say because we wouldn't look so different. "You and Daddy would speak more Chinese and you'd teach me and then we could speak Chinese to each other when we're around other people and nobody would understand."

I expected to imbue my children with Chinese culture. A former student of my husband's came to our house to teach us Chinese as a family. My children liked playing with her, but that was it. Then I organized a Chinese-language playgroup with a wonderful teacher. My kids had no interest in that either. Swimming? Oh sure, my little one is a fish. Skating? Absolutely. My older one drags me to the arena. Books — tons. Extra school — no. Not unless I forced them. I discovered that I didn't have what it took to make them go to either Chinese school or Hebrew school. I am equally negligent.

But they do love to celebrate Chinese holidays with food and decorations, family and friends. We get together with other Jewish families with children from China at Lunar New Year, the Autumn Moon festival, and occasions in between. Months ahead of time, my older daughter, the budding artist, will ask me about when we're going to the buffet at the Mandarin restaurant with them. Her eyes shine at the prospect of unlimited desserts and running around with the other kids.

I ask my younger daughter, hair in place with clips on either side and a ponytail just so, whether she likes being lots of things or if she'd prefer to just be one thing. She says, "Lots." And I'm not surprised by this, though I am relieved.

When my husband and I met we had different attitudes about identity. He was raised in a family of mixed background and no religion. They had chocolate for Easter and a box of *matzo* on the table for Passover. Potato *latkes* for Hanukah and Christmas presents. He was proud of this, proud of an identity of no-identity. At the time, I couldn't relate at all. I felt so totally Jewish, tied to my ancestors, part of an inevitable chain. I worried about my children and the confusion that they'd feel between their biological ancestors and mine.

But I didn't realize that somewhere along the way that chain would transmute into something entirely different. It was so much less vivid than my daily life with my children, my husband, and my own personal journey in experiencing the source of all light and love that comes with so many different names. My husband values diversity. As a kid, he learned to love studying plants and bugs in the ravine behind his house, where he wandered. And I've come to realize that my own identity is changeable, fluid, multifaceted, embracing far more than I'd ever have guessed.

What I've discovered is that a family is made up of individuals who, rubbing up against each other, each change their shape, the parents no less than the kids. So, curious about what else my younger daughter might add to her identity, I ask her whether she is anything else. She says, "Wisdom." Indeed, I won't argue with that. Anything else? "Cute," she says. Totally. Anything else? She turns to look at me, leaving her toys aside. "Family," she says.

"Being part of a family?" I ask.

"Yes," says my wise nearly six-year-old. "Having a family is the most specialest thing of all."

Psalm 8:3: "Out of the mouths of babes and sucklings have You ordained strength . . ."

"Face Your Fortune Bravely"

Sarah Giddens

"THAT'S RIDICULOUS," Shan shakes his shaggy black hair. "Even I could do better."

He returns to the completed survey in front of him. Curious about the offending answer, Yin Yin leans over his shoulder and I look over hers. Asked to recommend movies that parents adopting from China should see, one respondent suggests a particular Hong Kong action flick. Yin Yin is not so miffed.

"Have you ever seen Tony Leung?" she asks about the lead actor. "He's so cute."

"Yeah," I say. "Loved him in *Happy Together* and *Infernal Affairs*." Shan rolls his eyes.

We are in a classroom in downtown Toronto. Teenagers Shan and Yin Yin, recently from China and currently in my history class, have volunteered to translate a survey I've gathered from Chinese women. Shan and Yin Yin know that my daughter is from China and that I am interested in all things Chinese. They have generously offered to help me decipher the detailed answers that these women — about sixty recent immigrants to Canada — have just as generously provided.

Twenty minutes later Shan, pointing at some characters, erupts again.

"How stupid!"

This time it's question twenty-four: If an adopted child had a chance to visit China as an adult, which places of cultural importance do you think they should see? Someone wrote, much to Shan's dismay, that they should visit everywhere but Shanghai.

"Why not Shanghai?" Shan asks, waving his hands in exasperation.

"Maybe she thinks it's too Western, or maybe she had a boyfriend from Shanghai who dumped her," Yin Yin speculates.

For all their opinions and exclamations, Shan and Yin Yin have promised to translate character for word as precisely as possible. Sometimes the translated text reads a bit awkwardly. They've got electronic dictionaries, and for difficult characters, Shan will confer with his grandparents, the ones who keep him up late with impromptu revolutionary-era sing-alongs.

The generosity of these teenagers and of the women who have taken the time to reply is much more to me than a mere courtesy. They are helping me connect with my child's birth culture so that I, in turn, can help her find her place in it. And the nature and quality of their help tells me how much they care about our Chinese children and how happy they are to be able to explain their own culture.

Based on the year of my birth, in Chinese folklore I am a dog — *gou*. *Gou* is pronounced in the third tone, falling then rising, like the inside of a bowl. My husband is a tiger — *hu*, also the third tone. Our daughter is a tiger, too, or Tiger Girl — *hu niu*. Tigers and dogs, according to custom, make excellent companions. This pleases me because I cherish the threads that draw my family closer. While I lack information about my daughter's birth parents, I have found a way to learn about her roots and indulge another passion — collecting oral history.

I grew up in England, and one summer my mother took us to visit Canada. It was scary and exciting to travel far from home. Four years later when we immigrated to Canada, I felt lucky to know two countries and was certain that I wanted to see more. As an adult, I fashioned a mobile lifestyle supporting myself by teaching. The first experience was magical: I lived with a Kikuyu family in East Africa. Hanging out with Kenyans as I traveled the country after a term of teaching was doubly rewarding because I felt so at home. Invariably people would say, "You are from Canada but, ha, you sound like a Kikuyu."

I realized that a heady combination of friendship, history, and gossip can bind you to a place forever. I worked in Southern Africa, an Ojibwa reserve, a military base, and in Hong Kong — finding friends and making connections in each place. In 1997, I married Paul, settled in Toronto, and began the adoption process. Two years later, the Hefei Social Welfare Institute invited us to China. Flying home with baby Leah snuggled beside me, I felt such a strong desire to reach out and understand her birthplace that I wanted to get off the plane right then.

Back home, I tried to content myself with reading all manner of Chinese-related material, pondering the ways that mothers transmit culture. Yet, while I learned plenty, I still didn't feel as connected as I wanted to be. I wanted to give my daughter the tools for a fulfilling life, including an appreciation of her roots. At work I would daydream about questions that I wanted to ask women in China — as much to capture their voices and sentiments as to know their answers. The conversation that I most wanted to hear or read about — Chinese women talking about life in their own words — wasn't readily available. I set out to find a way to make that crucial connection and came up with a survey.

Thinking of questions came easily; I imagined I was posing them to a friend. Also, I thought about what I'd want to know if I were adopted. What I found difficult was censoring myself. Since I teach history, it was tough to refrain from probing about the impact of government policies on family life, for example. To keep on track, I asked other adoptive mothers what they most wanted to know. I kept in mind a tenet of questionnaire writing: make sure your survey will hold the interest of those who answer.

For help translating my questions into Chinese, I e-mailed an sos to my friend Cai Ying Feng, a.k.a. Cynthia, whom I met ten years ago in Shekou, across the border from Hong Kong. Funny and friendly, Cynthia used to loop her arm through mine as we strolled outdoors with our boyfriends. We had stayed in touch. Cynthia was from Hefei, like our daughter, and she had timed a visit there to coincide with our adoption trip. With her personal understanding of international adoption, Cynthia translated the questions into appropriate and — so I'm told — eloquent Chinese.

Initially, through friends, colleagues, and acquaintances, I distributed about sixty surveys to women born and raised in China who had recently come to Canada. At first I wasn't sure anyone would fill it in — each question was written in both languages so it was an intimidating eight pages long. Incredibly, almost every survey was returned, arriving in bundles from my students' parents, friends, and friends of friends, in the mailbox and over the Internet. The responses were so well-considered and heartfelt I decided to make it an ongoing project. (An English version of the survey is in the Appendix of this book, page 189.)

Photo by Catherine Farquharson

The surveys provide a snapshot of contemporary Chinese women, one that adoptive parents like me thirst for — even if members of the Academy of Social Sciences might have a fit over my methodology. What emerged was a portrait of a generous, thoughtful group of women who combined practical advice about raising daughters with obvious pride in their ancient culture — all delivered with sensitive concern for our children.

The respondents were mostly Northern and/or Eastern Chinese, had many siblings, and were often raised by grandparents. They were urban Mandarin speakers between the ages of thirty-six and fifty, mostly married with one son but wanting more children. It was an educated group, most with secondary school diplomas, about a third with bachelors, and a few with masters or doctorates. I'd assumed that anonymity would be important to women unaccustomed to making public their personal opinions, but some openly offered their time and friendship.

"It is a hard but great job to bring up a girl," one said.

"I want to help these parents," wrote another.

"I will leave my e-mail for connecting. I really want to make friends with you," someone else offered.

Most adoptive parents of Chinese girls place high value on exposing their kids to Chinese culture — but they might be surprised to find that the activities many of them favor are not necessarily the ones that my respondents would recommend. Assuming adopted children should grow up with an understanding of China, I asked the women, how would they rank various methods of doing just that? They chose from a list of eleven options, from learning the language to following current events. While the women ranked visiting China and learning history as most important, they thought learning holiday traditions and visiting the child's original orphanage were least important. It was, in short, the opposite of what many adoptive parents consider a priority. Perhaps the respondents believe children should know Chinese history and culture before they experience an orphanage visit.

Some Chinese have told me privately about the shame they feel when they see the impact of the one-child policy. "The most important thing to learn is Chinese history. What is happening in China has its historical reasons," one woman wrote, as if asking for our understanding. Most respondents, by the way, had heard about child abandonment by word of mouth and through the media. Some had seen it firsthand.

"In my village there were several children adopted. They were abandoned on the streets in front of the government gates. Some parents have to give the second child to others no matter the gender." But many said they did not learn about international adoptions until they left China.

An emphasis on learning about historical context came up again when respondents were asked where families should visit. Xian, the home of the terra-cotta warriors, was a favored site that would take our daughters far back to their roots in the Qin civilization. For the most part, the suggested itineraries fell into three groups not too far from the average tourist's path. Families should see Beijing, Hong Kong, Nanjing, Shanghai, and Xian, the women said. They should visit historical sites such as Tiananmen Square, the Great Wall, the former Imperial Palace, the Summer Palace, and Qufu, Confucius' hometown. They also recommended renowned spots of scenic or spiritual beauty such as the Huang Mountains, Tibet, the Shao Lin Temple, Guilin, and Inner Mongolia.

One respondent, clearly focused on helping adoptive families understand the economic basis for wrenching decisions, urged visits to the "the poorest, undeveloped villages e.g. villages in Gansu."

Parents often echo what they heard at home as children so I asked what kind of advice my Chinese respondents had heard. Their answers suggest the shadows of China's recent history — "Hope to have something to eat. Learn to endure hardships. Don't cry; it won't help" — as well as underscoring 2,500-year-old Confucian ideals. "Be industrious, honest, thrifty. Study hard so ancestors will be proud."

To get a sense of childhood in previous generations, I asked the women about role models, toys, and caregivers. The most popular heroes were: soldiers and revolutionaries, particularly Lei Feng, a selfless soldier who died young; Mao Zedong; Sun Zhongshan, "because he liberated women"; Lu Xun, "because he had deep thoughts, a sense of justice, and he is a patriot"; Liu Hu Lan, "who wasn't afraid of enemy soldiers and helped her people and died for them when she was only fifteen years old"; as well as the traditional tale of Mulan. Some respondents named relatives: "Grandpa — he was knowledgeable and had good eloquence." "My father — he was an accomplished painter and he had a very pleasant personality." "Mother — because she was kind and assiduous." Other role models were peers, with one respondent admiring "a classmate who is good at study," and "the classmate who was the top in school."

Childhood games were modest, reflecting aspects of culture — such as paper cut-outs — and economic conditions: "We didn't have toys. I collected wrapping paper, sand piles, and [played a] rubber band jumping game." Some play was familiar, such as riddles, skipping, and hide-and-seek, as were toys, such as building blocks and rag dolls. Shan and Yin Yin's diligent translation stumped me for a moment until I realized that "acting as family members" probably meant playing house.

The women had many ideas when asked for book suggestions. The most common novel recommended was Cao Xueqin's eighteenth-century *Dream of the Red Chamber*, while children were advised to enjoy histories as well as traditional and heroic tales: *The Monkey King, Hua Mu Lan, Fairy Tales, History of Chinese Taoism, The Three Kingdoms, Xi You Ji* or *West Traveling Journal, Jia Feng,* or *Family Story.* One title, *A Girl Selling Matches,* seemed familiar so I told Shan and Yin Yin about Paul and Leah weepily reading *The Little Match Girl.*

"Yeah, yeah," they said. "That's it."

The most popular title surprised me at first, translated by my teenaged volunteers as *"100,000 of Why."* I hit the Internet to discover an eight-volume science encyclopedia replete with questions such as, Why does the sun emit rays? *A Hundred Thousand Questions and Answers* was first published by Shanghai's People's Republic Publishing House in 1952, was revised in 1972, and has been read and apparently enjoyed by millions.

The list of suggestions for film, music, poetry, and art was so long and diverse that I could have spent weeks merrily Googling the titles. *Xiao Bin Zhang Ga,* a movie about a soldier helping the Red Army defeat the Japanese Army, was the most frequently recommended film. Shan and Yin Yin accepted without comment a mention of Liang Zhu, a violin soloist. *Erhu* (a traditional two-stringed guitar) and other folk instruments followed. A must-hear song? *Da Hai* or *Big Sea,* the first line of which, "Everywhere is my hometown," had been thoughtfully written out by someone keen to send a message to our children. Two popular cartoons, *Big-Head Son and Small-Head Dad* and *Three Buddhist Monks,* were also recommended. Apparently Tang-Dynasty-era poetry is the best, and the *Eight-horse Gallop* or any other paintings by artist Xu Bei Hong require a look-see.

The best advice you can give a person is to tell them to follow good advice. And the Mandarin idiom *"Cong Shan Ru Liu,"* meaning follow good advice as a river follows its course, captures that idea beautifully. What kind of advice, I wondered, might the women filling in the survey have for adoptive parents?

In many ways their words of wisdom tended to be the kind of sensible advice you'd hear in the playground, sprinkled with polite but urgent reminders to remember China.

"Don't see her as special Chinese kid; just nurture in the way you believe is best," said one as translated by my teen helpers.

"Don't forget Chinese history," advised another. "Let them study Western culture but encourage them to learn Chinese culture."

"Tell her Chinese historical stories. Let her participate in Chinese activities."

As for general childrearing, they recommended large quantities of love, tempered by limits.

"Give every possible minute to be with them. Give them a healthy, happy environment. Don't dote on her. Respect children's opinion." One instruction somewhat delightfully lost in translation was: "Inculcate the girl hardly and rigorously but do not spoil girl."

"Give true love and foster to become useful to society," one said. And, one that adoptive parents can all honor, "Love her like their born child."

One woman who offered no advice wrote, "I am curious about the reasons for adopting a Chinese child . . . I'm interested in knowing how you're going to explain the causes of abandonment, for if not properly conveyed she might develop a hatred instead of love toward China."

As I flipped through the surveys, I often felt at one with the respondents. I imagine this woman wrapping a warm blanket around our daughters: "Use your eyes to see China is developing and wish something good for China. Don't feel not-good about being Chinese. Please know about the population special rules that affect you. Hope, wish, you can love China."

More bracing was the advice the women offered our children. "Face life positively," one said. "Improve yourself in all aspects." Others wrote: "Face your fortune bravely." "Don't use money to measure everything." "Learn the virtues which the traditional Chinese girls have." "Combine Eastern and Western culture if possible." "Have ambition." "Place importance in sports and civil activity." "Be a good daughter to your parents." "Don't forget your roots and kindness of Canadian parents." "Love Canada and love China." "[I] hope you grow up in a happy family with good education and nurture and become a useful person in society."

The women did not hesitate to offer their final thoughts about the survey. Some were analytical: "This makes a strong relationship with Canada and China. The questions fitted the reality, have profound meaning, and reflect the society." Others had yet more advice: "Take a video in China of schools, factories, farms, hospitals — let them learn the real China to know that their motherland is a lovely country with industrious people."

"These parents love the child, they think of the other questions for them, and consider how to inculcate and how to let them remember where they are from — this is very good."

"Thank you, Chinese girls' Canadian parents," another wrote. "Hope the survey can help you and your children understand China."

My favorite comment? "You and your husband and your Chinese daughter are welcome to our place."

One of these parting shots sounded a little too much like — a parting shot. "Cudgel your brains," it began.

"What does this mean?" I asked Yin Yin.

"Oh," she replied, "'Cudgel your brains' means you really worked hard and paid attention to some problems. She thought the survey was good."

"That's a relief," I thought, rubbing my head.

Nice and Warm

Cindy Boates

THE RED-AND-BLACK SNOWSUIT seemed completely inappropriate as pajamas. A typical toddler snowsuit, it had padded pants with elastic top and legs and a red zippered jacket. Perfectly suited for the cold, though not frigid, Jiangxi winters though it may have been, it was definitely not the right sleepwear for a heated hotel room.

But wearing it to bed must have made sense to almost-three-year-old Lucy, sweating while she slept with the jacket on and zipped up to the collar. And it made perfect sense to me, too. The snowsuit was a gift from Zhu Mu Xiang, a woman living in a small village near Fuzhou, in Jiangxi province in southeastern China. In her own way, Lucy seemed to know that Mu Xiang was special to her, that the gift she had received just that day was something to be appreciated.

Lucy was probably born in or near Fuzhou. Found outside

a bustling marketplace, she was brought to the Fuzhou Social Welfare Institute the day after she was born in January 2002. Shortly after that, she was sent to Zhu Mu Xiang, who took care of Lucy in her home for the first six months of her life.

We were on our first "homeland visit," a return trip to China that has become increasingly popular among adoptive families. The trips are supposed to help our children understand their beginnings, reconnect with their homeland, and make their far-away birth country seem less mysterious. Homeland visits can include, as ours did, visits to the hometowns and social welfare institutes where our children had lived. An entire specialized travel industry has emerged to support the growing interest among adoptive parents to return to the places where their families were first formed and to explore China in a more leisurely way than is possible during the often stressful two-week adoption trip.

Adoption experts have written extensively about when is the right time in a child's life for a homeland visit. Some say that the orphanage visit shouldn't be too soon after the adoption or when the children are too young. Or they say that the visit should be combined with a fun cultural trip in order to first acclimatize the children so that they can be well-rested and prepared before they see and experience an orphanage.

That advice may work well for some but my job had given me an unusual opportunity to visit China while the girls were perhaps "too young" for a visit. I had been transferred to Manila for a two-year assignment in the Philippines. Since we were living in the same time zone, I wanted to take advantage of being close enough to make several trips to China, even though my daughters, Sophie, then age six, and Lucy, who was not yet three, were not "the right age." Sophie had a week off from school in November 2004, so we jumped at the chance to visit Lucy's hometown, Fuzhou, and Sophie's hometown, Gao'An, both in Jiangxi province.

I did try to prepare Sophie for what we were going to do and see, but she has never had a lot of questions about her beginnings, so I didn't prepare her much. And Lucy was too young to have much of an opinion one way or the other. So, ignoring the well-meaning advice about appropriate timing and preparedness, we were bound for China for a week.

Fuzhou is about 100 kilometers southeast of Nanchang, the capital of Jiangxi — an interesting ninety-minute drive through a semi-mountainous area, with pearl farms, a Buddhist temple, a few prosperous-looking private schools, and lots and lots of farmland alternating with clusters of ceramic-tiled homes and shops.

Our first stop in Fuzhou was at the orphanage itself. Like any obsessive adoptive parent, I had seen many photos of the building shared on the Internet by other families, so I recognized the distinctive green-mirrored building long before we turned into the driveway. The director in charge of adoptions gave us the grand tour of the buildings but we spent most of our time in the children's building. The charitable organization Half the Sky had recently been there, evidenced by newly renovated play-rooms, with pastel-painted walls covered in children's artwork and plentiful toys neatly lined up on the shelves. We toured the baby rooms, pausing for a look at a crib identified as the one that Lucy slept in once she left Zhu Mu Xiang's care and before she was taken to Nanchang to meet me. While we excitedly snapped photos, Lucy didn't seem particularly impressed by this crib over the dozen or so others, each with its tiny sleeping occupant. She seemed more interested in moving down the hall to the play-room where she could see and hear young toddlers and their caregivers playing.

Every orphanage maintains a file on each child who has spent time there. I have heard stories of additional interesting tidbits of information turning up in the orphanage file, such as a note or other object left with the baby by a birth parent. But we had no such luck: there was nothing there that I hadn't already seen.

With those formalities done, we hopped into a van, along with the director, and traveled the short distance to Zhu Mu Xiang's village. She and many of the other women living in the village often provide foster care to children from the Fuzhou SWI.

Lucy is a confident, outgoing kid, never sitting still and never at a loss for words. Except for that day. As soon as we arrived at the village, we were surrounded by a "welcoming committee" and Lucy was spooked by all the attention. After a couple of minutes, Mu Xiang arrived and wanted to take Lucy from my arms to hold her. But Lucy silently clung to me, as Mu Xiang's husband pointed to himself, saying "*yeye*" or grandfather. While of course I didn't expect Lucy to recognize her foster parents, I hadn't anticipated that she would react that way. It was overwhelming for all of us. We spent most of our visit inside Mu Xiang and *Yeye*'s small brick home, which seemed to consist of a kitchen, a bedroom with a large television, and a center room with little furniture but for a Christian altar that seemed oddly out of place. (I later discovered that the village is home to a small pocket of Christian converts who follow the indigenous Three-Self Patriotic Movement.) Visitors wandered in and out, to check us out and to squeeze Lucy's cheeks and pat Sophie's head.

Then came the exchange of gifts, always a part of social interaction in China. Although we brought a few small items, I later felt they were woefully inadequate when I saw what Mu Xiang had bestowed on Lucy: several small yogurt drinks, some fabulously sweet Nanfeng oranges, and a silver cross necklace, which she placed around Lucy's neck, while pointing to the portrait of Jesus on her bedroom wall. And, of course, the Red Snowsuit. But none of this warmed Lucy's heart yet: she still wouldn't let go of me.

Mu Xiang also stuffed a small treasure into my hand, a small red purse, which contained her name, address, and phone number, all neatly written in Chinese and English.

Other foster mothers popped in and out of the house during our visit, each with a baby in her arms or straddling a hip. As I looked around at the other small children, I couldn't help but think about when Lucy was one of them, clinging to Mu Xiang, before the amazing chain of events that brought us together. And I also wondered about the future of these children. Where would they end up? Would they find permanent families soon, in China or elsewhere, or would they spend years in this village before heading out into the world on their own?

Our all-too-short visit came to an end. As the entourage walked us back to our van, Mu Xiang was in tears saying goodbye. Our first visit ended with her walking away from our van crying. A little too late, Lucy finally found her voice to call out the window in her best playgroup Mandarin, "*Zaijian*, goodbye, I'll be back later." But I doubt Mu Xiang heard it.

Back in the security and comfort of the van, Lucy had a lot to say.

"The lady," she began.

"What about the lady?" I asked.

"The lady was crying."

"Why was she crying?"

"She's sad."

"Why is she sad?"

"She wants to pick me up."

On some level, Lucy understood that the visit was significant. And when we got home after dinner, she decided she needed to put on that Red Snowsuit. Maybe it was her own way of saying, "Thanks, it was nice to see you." Then, totally exhausted, she fell asleep.

Fortunately, we had gone to Sophie's hometown first before we visited Lucy's. Had we headed for Gao'An after our Fuzhou visit, Sophie might have been expecting the same flurry of activity. Not that we were not welcomed in Gao'An — because we were — but it was a much less emotional visit.

Gao'An, about 100 kilometers southwest of Nanchang, is a smaller, less developed city on the Jin River, the focal point of the city. A floating footbridge built from wooden rowboats tied together crosses the river. We spent a long time just meandering back and forth across the footbridge, admiring an ornate watchtower that appeared to be recently built, watching people fish and wash their laundry in the river, but mostly answering questions about who we were and why we were there. Strangely, a Russian circus troop was also in town so some people assumed we were involved with the circus.

The Gao'An Social Welfare Institute is near the watchtower, in a traditional old village slated for destruction as part of long-term urban renewal. Across the street, a rice noodle factory was in full swing, with dozens of long stranded bundles of rice noodles drying in the courtyard on the "rice noodle trees."

The Gao'An orphanage is smaller and older than Fuzhou's but features a homey layout, sectioned into small self-contained "apartments," each housing three babies and a nanny, complete with a playroom, bathroom, and a sitting room with a television. However, it was almost devoid of toys. Many of the children were fostered out so only the very young were in the orphanage, each in a sturdy wooden crib. There was one fancy metal crib, painted pink. The director pointed to it, saying that this would have been the crib that Sophie slept in. Never mind that I had been told that Sophie had lived with a foster family up until the day before she was adopted; it really meant something to her that she had slept right there, that this was "her bed."

As we had at Lucy's orphanage, we went through Sophie's orphanage file but found no new information. We had no luck finding Sophie's foster mother, either. When we asked, the director pulled out a well-worn book on his desk and flipped to a page. "She has moved away."

That was lesson number one about timing that first visit to the orphanage: if you wait too long, the trail might grow cold. Lucy was adopted two years before our first visit. People at the Fuzhou SWI still remembered her, the director remembered me, and her foster mother could still be traced. But at Sophie's SWI, the orphanage director had changed, her foster mother had moved away, as had the woman who found her. The closest we got was finding the man who signed as witness to Sophie's finding, but he now denied that he had. Nobody there really remembered her — too much time had passed: almost six years. If we had waited much longer, we thought, the orphanage itself might have been gone — it was slated to be moved to a new building and the old building was going to be torn down. We did visit Sophie's abandonment site, or "finding place" as some parents prefer. It was a school, so not much had changed. But when we looked for another family's site, it simply wasn't there anymore. It had been in a market under a bridge, but by the time we arrived the bridge had been expanded and the market was gone.

In another few years, who knows what changes will have occurred to further alter or eliminate these landmarks. Even if we work hard at keeping up a relationship with the orphanages by sending letters and photos, it will not prevent the bricks and mortar — and the memories — from disappearing.

Luckily for us, less than two years passed before we returned for our second homeland visit in April 2006, and not too much had changed yet in either city.

In Gao'An, no one had yet torn down the old orphanage

building. The noodle factory was still in full operation, and the center of town was still the old footbridge across the Jin River.

In Fuzhou, there were a couple of glitzy new hotels, but otherwise the place looked much the same. But when we got to the foster-mother village outside town, we discovered that Zhu Mu Xiang had achieved hero-status — not only was she the only foster mother who had had a return visit from one of her children, but now she had been visited twice.

This time, Lucy was looking forward to the visit — by now, she was over four years old and already skilled in the art of sibling one-upmanship ("I have a foster mother and you don't.")

Lucy bounded ahead of us as we were greeted by the entire village. Mu Xiang's tiny house filled with other foster mothers, each with a baby in her arms, and each thrusting photos into my hand — pictures of children they once looked after and forever wondered about.

Courtesy Cindy Boates

We were more prepared this time for the gift exchange. We brought a photo album filled with pictures of Lucy, a pearl necklace, Philippine snacks, and a purse. Lucy, who had assisted in the wrapping of the gifts back at the hotel, was now busily assisting in the unwrapping. She helped put the pearl necklace on Mu Xiang and told long stories describing each photo in the album. In return, Lucy was given shoes, more clothes, and a big orange-and-white stuffed dog whose eyes lit up and played a catchy Chinese techno-pop tune. But no sweet Nanfeng oranges this time — wrong season.

Best of all, this visit ended with a beaming Lucy getting a piggyback ride back to the van by her foster mother.

"*Zaijian*, goodbye, I'll be back later." And she will.

A Month in Beijing

Glen McGregor

MY DAUGHTER CLEO tilted her head up to the straw hanging from the top of her fruit drink and took a long sip as she considered my question. She looked around the patio restaurant before answering.

"I guess I like Beijing because everyone here looks like me," she said.

After three weeks in China, it was the response my wife and I had hoped to hear. But even then, we weren't sure if she was just parroting back our own line. Before we left Canada, we had told Cleo that for once, her white parents would be the racial minority. In their birth country, she and her little sister, Scarlet, would blend in. That, at least, was the idea when we decided to take a six-week holiday in China.

What we didn't understand was how foreign we really were.

When we adopted Cleo five years earlier, we had pledged to

keep Chinese culture in her life. Taking our holiday in China, we hoped, would send a strong signal to the girls that we valued the country and culture in which they were born. But in truth, that was secondary. Our experience on our two adoption trips was so exhilarating that we wanted a rerun. We craved the giddy sensation unique to international adoption — the thrill of foreign travel combined with becoming a parent.

It was not, we found, a sentiment shared by all adoptive parents. Shortly before we left, I mentioned our trip to another father who had adopted two children from China. He was stunned that we would voluntarily travel to Asia.

"Why go there when you can visit EPCOT?" he asked. On his family's adoption trips, he said, he had spent as much time as possible in the hotel and ventured out only on daily outings with an English-speaking tour guide to sights like the Great Wall or the Forbidden City.

Other adoptive families we knew were planning "homeland tours." But, for us, after two adoption trips, the idea of another guided tour held little appeal. Instead, my wife decided to enroll in a language school in Beijing for a month to develop her Mandarin. She would go to school during the day while I would look after the girls. I would be a stay-at-home dad to Cleo, then five, and Scarlet, eighteen months. After her language program, we would take a cruise down the Yangtze and make a short visit to Hunan, their home province.

On a March afternoon, we dragged the girls through the modern corridors of the Beijing airport and arrived at the customs hall. We waited in line as an official in an olive uniform checked passports. The girls, still bleary from the hours of air travel, looked nervous. Cleo rode in the stroller with her arms wrapped around her sister, who sat on her lap. I knelt down to once more repeat the assurance we had offered them many times before the trip:

we were just *visiting* China, they would be coming home with us. Children think magically, and it was possible the girls might believe we were taking them back to their birthplace for good. But clutching my children's Canadian passports, on the threshold of legal entry to their home country, it was me who needed to quell the irrational fear. Of course, they were mine forever. China would never rescind an adoption, I told myself.

We had rented an apartment in a modern building in Wu Dao Kou, a dense neighborhood in the north of Beijing near several universities. It was decorated in the contemporary Chinese style; that is, sparsely furnished but needlessly opulent, with the barren marble floors fitted with inlaid heating. Out our window, we could see ranks of Soviet-style apartment blocks and an even less spectacular view of the Pizza Hut across the street.

Still jet-lagged, we woke at 4:00 a.m. on the first morning and looked down through the dawn as delivery men steered through the streets with giant loads balanced on bicycles. Later, we began a routine that we would follow almost every day. I ran down to a take-out restaurant on the street and brought back a plastic bag full of *baozi,* a steamed bun filled with spiced meat. After breakfast, my wife left for her language lessons, and I packed up the girls. Cleo rode in the stroller, and Scarlet went in the backpack child-carrier, peering out over my shoulder. I tucked a batch of diapers and a *Rough Guide to China* in the pouch underneath her and headed for the elevator. So began our daily adventures.

Outside our building, the street noise enveloped us. Step off a plane in Asia and you immediately recognize its smell. But China has its own sound, too, a flavor of car horns, store loudspeakers, and, in our neighborhood, the fruit sellers who endlessly repeated the phrase, "*Yi kuai, yi kuai, yi kuai,*" (the price of one Chinese yuan for a chunk of pineapple on a stick).

Each journey kicked off with the adrenaline pump of crossing the street. Few aspects of urban life in China felt as foreign as the traffic. In Beijing and just about everywhere else we visited, cars and trucks commanded the right of way over pedestrians and bicycles. Even those pushing children must yield or risk certain injury. More than once, I had to yank the stroller back onto the curb like a bullfighter.

On the other side of the intersection was our launch pad, the Wu Dao Kou light-rail terminal. As we arrived, a sleek new European commuter train glided into the station. I slid the stroller through the doors and felt a tingle of travel buzz. With all of Beijing just a subway connection away, where would we go? Tiananmen, the Forbidden City, the Pearl Market, the Temple of Heaven?

First, we had to transfer from our train to Beijing's main subway loop. Even with the 2008 Olympics fast approaching, the subway system built under Mao's direction was still horribly antiquated. At the Xizhimen station, our main transfer point, there were no elevators or escalators. We had to descend a five-storey staircase, with Scarlet on my back and Cleo and her stroller in my arms. I stopped at the first landing, wheezing, and realized I would have to do the same thing on the way back, except going up instead of down.

After another flight of stairs, we were on a platform so crowded that I clung to a pillar as the morning rush flowed around us. I felt the gaze of hundreds of commuters' eyes.

On our two previous trips to China, we saw the interest that white parents with Chinese babies stirred in public, particularly when visiting the rural province from which both our daughters had come. In Beijing, we expected a more cosmopolitan reaction. Foreigners, after all, were common in the capital, and since many adoptive families passed through the city on their way home, white parents with Chinese children wouldn't seem so outlandish, we thought.

But inside Beijing's subway stations and on the trains, other passengers stared openly. Their eyes darted from the girls to me and back again. Some would whisper about us in Mandarin. I quickly learned to pick up the phrase *Zhongguo haizi* — Chinese children. Cleo noticed, too, and soon began to bristle. Our promise that she would blend in wasn't bearing out.

During the day, the girls and I were in near constant motion. One trip took us to the zoo to look at the macaque monkeys and the depressed pandas pacing their enclosure. On another, we went to the aquarium with its moving sidewalk that runs through a tunnel at the bottom of the tank. On another, we shopped for shoes in an indoor mall with a near infinite variety of children's footwear.

But the real adventures were unplanned and away from the tourist sites. We strolled for hours through the *hutong* alleys, with Cleo shrieking about the stench from the communal toilets. Some days we spent the morning looking at hanging meat or fresh vegetables in the outdoor markets. Others were consumed by my ongoing search for Cultural Revolution souvenirs, picking through antique stores full of dusty Mao busts and photos of Zhou Enlai. We were *flâneurs* in an ancient city, and the more we walked, the more we wanted to keep going.

Eventually, we would find a restaurant and break for lunch. After a week, I had assembled a gazetteer of restaurant Mandarin. *Bu tai la* — not too spicy, was repeated often. Cans of pop — a lapse in parenting, I admit — came with the command *Liang ge shui bi,* two Sprites. *Mai dan* requested the check, which was almost always laughably small.

After lunch, a visit to the park. Most neighborhoods had small outdoor gyms with blue-and-yellow painted metal pipes that, back home, would have signified play structures. In Beijing, these were fitness clubs designed for seniors. We went to them anyway. The girls would clamber over the elliptical machines while I'd field questions from curious grandparents. I had learned a few Mandarin phrases to explain adoption. Although my comprehension was rudimentary, I soon learned to anticipate the pattern of the questions they would invariably ask. Yes, they're Chinese. Yes, they're sisters. No, their mother isn't Chinese. We're all Canadian. Then, if the inquisitor was particularly brave, more questions about the birth mothers.

Back in Canada, our family had agreed that details of the girls' origin were their own business. At our local grocery store in Ottawa, total strangers in the checkout line would ask whether Cleo was adopted. I would reply with an equally impertinent question: "Were your kids born vaginally or by Caesarian?"

In Beijing, I spoke more freely of the girls' personal histories. Somehow, it felt like China was in on it, the adoption thing, although most Beijingers seemed clueless about the thousands of children abandoned every year.

Early in our trip, I relished the conversations with strangers. I was getting a chance to practice Mandarin, and the thrill I felt on our adoption trips was back again. The girls were less impressed. Bashful in the first few encounters, Cleo began to resent the constant questions and particularly disliked curious onlookers feeling her skin. She began to make faces at them and eventually asked my wife to teach me the phrase for "Please don't touch her."

In the evenings, we returned by train to the Wu and met my wife for dinner at a restaurant near our apartment. We became regulars in a busy diner popular with university students. The décor was decrepit, but the food was cheap and sensationally good. We gorged on Beijing duck and green beans smothered in garlic, all the better with seventy-five-cent quarts of beer. While we ate and talked, the waitresses entertained the girls, taking Scarlet to see the fish tanks in the lobby or letting Cleo into the kitchen to take pictures of the ducks that hung from the ceiling.

One day when my wife stayed home from school with a head cold, I went into our restaurant to order a bowl of soup for takeout. They didn't have a Styrofoam bowl large enough, so one of the waiters we knew offered to bring a porcelain bowl up to our apartment, serve the soup, and return with the empty bowl. It seemed like too much effort, but he insisted. As we left the restaurant, I was horrified at the colonial scene we had created: a Westerner marching along the street, while a Chinese guy in a brocaded red tunic followed, a respectful two paces behind, carrying a giant urn of soup. In the days of the Boxer Rebellion, I'd have been shot for creating the sight.

By our fourth week in the city, we had fallen into a happy pattern. It was still a fantasy life — neither of us was working and we were still burning cash at about the same rate we did at home — but we began talking about the possibility of one day living in China permanently.

Not long after, on a crowded subway platform, I noticed a young woman carrying a child in her arms. During the day, most

Courtesy Glen McGregor

subway riders were on their way to work. It was unusual to see other parents with children. I leaned on the handles of Cleo's stroller and gave the woman a friendly smile. She muttered something at us. I couldn't pick up the words but the tone was clearly unfriendly. Odd, I thought, as I watched her carrying the six-year-old through the doors. I noticed she didn't have a stroller, and it occurred to me that I never saw other parents with strollers, either.

Then, a chilling realization: parents didn't need strollers because no one had more than one child. The girls and I were an oddity not just because I was a white man with Chinese children, or because I was a father alone in public with his daughters — something I rarely saw in Beijing. We stood out because we were a family with two children. The woman who had hissed at me on the subway platform resented it. The same one-child policy that let us and thousands of other Westerners adopt from China kept her from having another child.

One night shortly before we left Beijing, we took the subway down to Tiananmen Square. On any visit to China's symbolic center, it's hard not to first think of the tanks and the students. But on this warm spring evening, there was no hint of menace. Tiananmen was crowded with families strolling under the artificial lights that made the square glow. Children lined up to buy ice cream while their parents tried to launch kites. Chinese tourists posed for photos and even the stone-faced soldiers who patrol the square seemed at bit more at ease that evening. We bought two dragon-shaped paper kites from a street vendor and gave them to the girls.

Next to Mao's tomb, my daughters raced over the paving tiles, dragging their kites and screaming with delight as they tried to force them into the air. Cleo stopped and pulled on the string, and the light wind finally bit. Her kite rose up. I helped her let out some slack and the dragon zigzagged above us.

She fed it more string and soon the kite became another white dot among the dozens of others in the night. The country that had given our family its two greatest gifts had slipped us another tiny perfect moment.

Just Known as Me

Jasmine Bent

TO ME, BEING ADOPTED is as normal as the sun being bright. I do not have any memories from before I was here in Canada with my family. All I know is my perfectly normal and happy life. Therefore, I don't understand why it is that people think being adopted makes you different.

I don't remember a single moment when I did not know I was adopted. For me, it is just a part of who I am. Never have I woken up and looked in the mirror and thought to myself "Jasmine, you are adopted." Being adopted doesn't make me feel particularly special. Shooting bull's-eyes on a target in a biathlon, laughing over inside jokes with my friends, or just hanging with my mom — those are things that make me feel special.

Do people see me differently? Well, maybe some curious strangers and the odd nosy neighbor. However, especially now that I am in high school, other teenagers don't know that I am adopted and, if they do know, they don't care. The only people who do know are the ones I choose to tell, and for the most part they ask a few questions and then don't mention it again. At school I'm just known as me, not the adopted girl or anything else like that. I live in a racially diverse area. The one thing I do notice is that in high school, you end up being friends with mostly people of your own race. I can't relate to any of the first-generation Chinese girls, but I have a lot of girlfriends who are second generation. I find that Canadian-born Chinese girls often have more similar interests in music and books, as well as similar fashion tastes. Most of my friends who are second generation can speak Chinese, however, they rarely do, except to their parents. My guy friends are mostly Caucasian. Outside of school I have almost all Caucasian friends.

People ask me whether or not I'm embarrassed about having white parents, and truthfully, I'm just embarrassed having *my* parents. My dad: I love him dearly, but he does not understand the word "cool" in any way. I can distinctly remember him holding up a pair of "granny panties" insisting I buy that kind of underwear rather than the more normal undies I was looking at. He actually was chasing me around the store with grandma panties!

My mother is usually pretty good; however, at my age you try to be seen with your parents as little as possible. I don't mind that my mom can't cook the best dumplings or egg rolls, because, well, none of my friends' parents can either. I'm glad that my parents aren't traditional Chinese parents, who often seem to put a lot of pressure on their children to be perfect at everything academic and who seem to think that leisure activities are not important. I have lots of pressure in my life already, and I'm glad my parents support me and want me to do my best but are not too hard on me.

With that being said, life when I was younger would have been easier if I looked like my parents. It was about grade 3 or 4 when kids really started to notice that there was something different about my family. I often felt annoyed about having to explain adoption over and over to my peers.

Many adoptive parents insist on exposing their children to a variety of different cultural experiences, as my parents did. When I was little, I attended Chinese school as well as Chinese culture camp. The only thing I liked was the food at the parties. I also participated in the Chinese martial art of kung fu. However, when I was about twelve and had a choice about whether to attend or not, I stopped going to all three.

Chinese culture has never interested me any more or less than the cultures of any other country. To this day I am dragged to every event the Chinese Embassy holds and every party for arriving Chinese delegates. It's usually boring because there are no other people my age.

I would love to go back and visit China one day. I think it would be interesting to visit my orphanage, just to see where I lived before I came to Canada. I would also like to see the tourist attractions. The Great Wall of China would be on my list. However, if I could only choose one — sightseeing or visiting my orphanage — I would choose sightseeing. To me, my orphanage is just like an old house I used to live in but have no memories of. I don't think I would look for my birth parents, although I would consider putting an article in the newspaper, just to let them know that I am happy, healthy, and loved. In a special way, I definitely do have a love for my birth parents, for giving me life and a chance for a future, but it's a different love than the one I have for my parents. I love my parents because they have taken care of me as far back as I can remember, and I love my biological parents for giving me life.

My adult life seems so far away, although the years are flying past. I'll be turning sixteen on my next birthday. I'm very excited to try out different courses in school to find a possible career choice. Right now, I am exploring the option of working in the mission field. I'm preparing to leave on my first mission trip shortly to Monterrey, Mexico. I know that I will come back with new experiences and new ideas. I really wanted to go on this trip, to help others as well as to feel that I have accomplished something in my life that is meaningful to God. Other careers I have considered are journalism and law. I have no doubt that I will continue exploring different career areas that will appeal to me in different experiences.

Adoption is not a big issue currently in my life. I have found that now that I am older and my schedule is very busy, I do not even think about it. When I was younger I had a much harder time, just because other little kids were curious and asked me too many questions. It was often frustrating because many times I didn't know what to say. Being older and more educated about adoption now, I would probably find explaining it easier.

Yes, being adopted is a part of who I am but it is just one part of a very complex being!

A Long Way from Hunan

Lia Calderone

FOR MY SIXTEENTH BIRTHDAY last month, I had a Hawaiian-themed barbecue with my family and friends around the backyard pool. Unfortunately, my friends Louise, Aimee, and Seiyan couldn't be there for the chocolate fountain or the swimming, so the night before my party, we had a sleepover at my house. After they arrived around 1 p.m., we decided to go shopping at the mall. We browsed for a while at different stores. I bought a new top at H&M, Aimee bought a necklace, and Louise bought a purse. After supper, we watched *Ghost Rider* and *Freedom Writers*.

We talked about the provincial exams we had recently taken, because we had all just finished grade 10, although at different schools. We were happy that summer had finally started. We were also glad we had decided to get together again, since the last time we had seen each other was in April.

We're like any other group of teenage girls, but we also share a special history. The four of us lived in the same orphanage in the Chinese province of Hunan, an area known for its spicy foods and for being the birthplace of Chairman Mao Zedong. We've had these get-togethers, along with another girl, Audreanne, since our parents adopted us from China.

Hanging out with my Hunan friends is an example of what being adopted from China is like for me. It doesn't make me feel different at all. Whether I'm shopping or watching movies, adoption just doesn't seem like a big deal. Just like my brown eyes and brown hair, it's a part of me.

After hearing my last name, which obviously isn't a typical Chinese name, many people ask about my nationality. I tell them I was born in China, but I was adopted and my parents are both Italian. The next question is usually, "So, do you know who your real parents are?" I understand that they mean biological parents, but I remind them that the parents I live with are my real parents. I tell them that I don't know the identities of my biological parents. I've never really wondered about my biological parents. Teachers notice, while doing roll call, that my last name isn't Chinese. One teacher even asked me if I was Filipina, because he thought my last name sounded Spanish. I don't become angry or offended when people comment about my last name or my appearance. I just tell them that I'm adopted from China and my parents are Italian and then answer any questions that follow.

When I was four years old, we moved to China for two years. One of my first remarks when we arrived, my mother told me, was that there were a lot of Chinese people there. We went to China to adopt my sister Alissa, who was also from Hunan. Alissa is more curious than I am and has recently asked whether we can find her biological parents. My parents have told her that they would do what they could, but that it would be difficult.

I did kindergarten in China and I was able to speak and write in Chinese like the other boys and girls. I remember having rice and fish sticks for lunch and then having a nap on the bunk beds. Since I was so young, I don't remember a lot. I do remember the time our apartment kitchen started flooding. The man my parents phoned for help only spoke Chinese, so I had to explain the situation.

When we returned to Canada, I went to a bilingual school. I took Chinese lessons for a bit, but eventually I stopped. I lost the ability to speak Chinese when I was learning to speak French at school and Italian with my grandparents. Sometimes I regret not continuing my lessons, because it's fun to be able to speak different languages and it's part of my culture. I can speak more Japanese than Chinese now because of my karate lessons. I can count, name different body parts and karate strikes, and use simple, polite sentences. I find Japanese and Chinese are difficult languages to learn, because I can't relate the words to another language. So it's all memory. I can understand Italian, for example, because I can relate it to French.

There are about a dozen Chinese kids out of about 150 students in my grade at school, and I'm friends with a few of them. I have fewer Chinese friends than Caucasian friends. The group of kids I hang out with on Friday nights aren't Chinese. They were all born in Quebec, with different backgrounds. They all know I was adopted and it has never affected our relationships. They've never treated me differently or unfairly. It hasn't stopped me from seeing movies, or going out for dinner at a new restaurant, or hanging out at school with them. I have a close friend from elementary school who was also adopted, but not from China. She was from Romania and her parents have also adopted other children from Colombia. At karate, I have numerous close friends, whom I also spend a lot of time with. Whether at competitions, regular training, barbecues, or just hanging out, whether they

are Caucasian or Chinese, being adopted or not doesn't affect my relationships with them.

My parents have asked my sister and me if we would like to go to China next summer to see the 2008 Beijing Olympics. I think it would be an amazing experience to watch the Olympics, visit the orphanage I lived in for four months, and learn more about the country where I was born. Although I saw the Great Wall when I was younger, that would still be an attraction I'd wish to see again. I think it'd be interesting and important to return to the country where I was born because it's part of my life. I'd also like to see the different lifestyle.

Adoption isn't a big issue in my life. I'm a teenage girl, so I have other things on my mind, like school and friends. Being adopted doesn't prevent me from being a normal teenage girl and doing the things I like to do. Instead, I think it has given me different opportunities. If I hadn't been adopted, my life would probably be completely different. I might not have learned to play the piano, which I have been playing for four years. Perhaps I wouldn't have discovered karate, my favorite sport. I've been doing karate for nine years — more than half my life — and I received my black belt in August 2006. I cannot imagine having different friends! And most important, I would not have wanted a different family. We definitely have our arguments, sometimes about the smallest things, but we also have a lot of laughs. I cannot imagine living with another family. I don't think anyone could care for me and love me the way they do. I'm extremely happy with my life and unbelievably happy that my parents adopted me. I wouldn't have wanted it any other way.

Our Silk Road

Douglas Hood

LIKE A PAIR of Kerouac vagabonds, Suki and I have lugged our satchels to a lot of low-end hotels and have killed a lot of time in bus stations and on ferries. We've wandered the empty streets of towns where tourists won't go, eaten at tortilla stands, hired taxis or even the hotel clerk for the day with the hope of finding a local gem. We understand this is what we do and we know the price. While we rarely make it to neighborhood cookouts, we might be rooting for the bull at a bullfight, getting lost trying to find an orphanage, forking over $25 for a taco in Zurich, or perhaps flopping in a hotel room at noon in a jet-lagged stupor. Even Suki's passport looks like it slept in a park. Her daddy is afflicted with wanderlust.

If she runs her finger down the old Pan American highway from Nome to Punta Arenas, Suki comes to the realization she's been to every state, lake, or province that it touches. Whether landing on a strip in the jungle and being met by an Indian in a canoe, or in the sixteenth arrondissement in Paris, we carry no guides, maps, or reservations. We ask a lot of questions and use good old-fashioned fear to get by. The first day can be a downer with three empty weeks staring at us, but by the last day we can be teary, kissing some family goodbye.

A lot of it is not easy but over time I see the payoff — our bond and her sense of place in the world. Suki is aware of the difference between Slovenia and Slovakia, and that you can only get to Andorra by bus, and that in Iceland you can run a race at midnight. She knows that the roads across Mongolia are teeth-rattling, and that you can ask immigration officers in Cuba not to stamp your passport. She did the legwork for our book on the terra-cotta warriors, ate dumplings with her orphanage director, and put her foot over the border of Paraguay before our taxi driver sped us to the safety of Brazil. She's seen the eyes of Guatemalan sisters taking their first elevator ride and going to their first movie. No wonder she got bored on a cruise.

Our calendar warns me of an end to this grand journey. My baby is sixteen now and the advice pouring in tells me to prepare her for the real world. SATS are more real than Burma, volunteer hours in the library are worth more than the Siberian Rail. Have I done the right thing?

Okay, okay, I got an A for Geography, but how would I be scored on my original contract to be a mummy and daddy in North Haven? I'll get no ballots for the hall of fame. Right from day one I couldn't get through *Goodnight Moon* without a yawn, and I lasted through maybe eighty pages of *Harry Potter*. Yes, that was me snoring in the car with sports radio on while she was swinging in the playground or dashing into Stop & Shop. No, I never baked cupcakes. And I probably overdosed her on spaghetti. I didn't teach her to sew a button, do tie-dye, or put on lipstick. I confess that I told her to ignore the darks and whites in the wash.

Courtesy Douglas Hood

I dressed her up as a ladybug for the Halloween party in kindergarten, only to have the teacher block us at the door. It was the wrong day. I had no stomach for the PTA and only grudgingly showed up at her band concerts and parades. Helpless, I let other moms pick out her gown for the spring dance. I have no idea where she gets her bras. Let's see, did I mention menstruation? As for the birds and bees, the school did that, right?

She battled problems, and I ask myself, did I not do enough? There were two ear operations, a GI bleed, a scoliotic back, bunions that bent her feet to the point of pain. Every winter she filled the sink with her nosebleeds. I blamed myself and cried for a day for missing her slipped epiphysis (this one requires a pin in the hip — turns out they read the film wrong, a near miss).

Was it my laissez-faire approach that led to one of those "Are you the father of . . . ?" calls from American Eagle Outfitters, or that caused her clarinet to go *pffft* during the music final? Because I never read enough to her, is that why her only "books" are *People* magazine? Why her essays are in a mix of English and instant messaging? Is it my fault that when I explain a word like *abstruse,* she tells me, "Daddy, I can't learn one more word!" while chiming the lyrics to Eminem? Oh, the weight and guilt of parenthood; especially flying alone, you have no one else to blame.

While most families were happy having their Sunday picnics and playing Pictionary, I had Suki training for the Special Forces. I propped her up on cross-country skis at four. Soon she was doing laps around the block, her marathoner dad logging her splits with a stopwatch. By eight, she was helping me in class teaching students how to do a spinal tap. Then she was on to triathlons. By twelve she had "suffered" through the last of the American Film Institute's top 100 films (all black-and-white, she protested). Two years later it was a woodworking class with retired men making furniture. And on her sixteenth birthday, she reluctantly took the bow with blistered ol' Dad in the stern in the Adirondack Canoe Classic, ninety miles of rivers and stormy lakes against 300 other rabid kayakers and "war" canoeists. What did Nietzsche say: "What doesn't destroy me makes me stronger"? Tell her that.

Sooner or later the drill guy gives in, the guard changes. She blossomed from the little girl who could never, ever beat me at anything — except maybe finding quarters under the seat — to the young woman who programs my cell phone, tells me not to wear that shirt with that tie, hands me the lighter bag, and yes, the final blow, outdashes me to the car. She mercilessly patted my belly and asked, "What happened, Daddy?" I hung up a faded picture of a trimmer me winning a race and countered by telling her, "Wait 'til you're sixty."

Finally independence arrives, but, for me, not with celebration. For our first six years I never went a ten-hour stretch without her. I even mowed the yard holding her hand. When I got called into work late at night, I pulled her out of bed and propped her up on the car seat like *Weekend at Bernie's*. Now I'm relegated to walking fifty paces behind her at her high school. It's getting worse. Like today, she's in Spain and it's been five days since I have heard from her. I gaze at her room with its posters and teddies. I'm following the advice and "letting go."

The phone rings and it's Suki in Salamanca. She'll be there for a month to learn Spanish, get some European culture, test being away from home, and maybe find her first little romance.

"Hi, Dad."

"Suki, are you having a good time?" I prepped myself not to be angry.

"Yeah."

"Do you have friends?"

"Yeah, lots."

"How's school?"

"Okay."

"And the family house you're staying in?"

"I just eat and sleep there."

"Suki, I need to hear from you. It's been since Saturday."

"I sent an e-mail."

"E-mail? I didn't get it."

"Maybe I didn't. Sorry. What are you doing?"

"Me? Not much. I miss you." I'm thinking of the empty days before Suki.

"I love you, Daddy." Those days are coming back.

I look out the window over my desk and I can see Suki, as she does each September, leading her high school swim team out of the locker room for a meet. They perform their cheers. You ask me, Suki is the loudest. Suki is in the medley relay, one of the four best swimmers. She does her leadoff signature backstroke, puts them in a slim lead, the butterflyer dives in, and Suki leans close to the water, screaming. The last one, the freestyler, touches the wall and the girls embrace and dance over their narrow win.

Across the pool, I get a smile and wave from my girl. I smile too. Because when they placed that little four-year-old on my lap in Hangzhou, this is what I envisioned.

Appendix
Women and Chinese Culture Survey

Dear Reader,

I am a Canadian teacher who, with my husband, adopted a beautiful baby girl from Eastern China in 1999. Since then, I have met many other adoptive parents who are keen to better understand Chinese culture.

The purpose of this informal survey is to gather information about the roles of women in China in order to share it with adoptive families in Canada. Your insight will help us understand Chinese gender and adoption issues.

I kindly request women from China who now live in Canada to fill in this survey. Please answer as many questions as possible. You do not need to provide your name or address. However, if you are willing to talk to me or if you would like to receive the results of this survey, please contact me at: sarahgiddens2@hotmail.com.

Thank you very much,
Sarah Giddens BA, BEd, MEd

General Information

1. What is your age? (circle one)

   a. <20   b. 20–35   c. 36–50   d. 51–65   e. 66+

2. What is your highest level of education?

   _____

   (e.g., primary, secondary, diploma, bachelor, masters, doctorate)

3. What is your marital status?

   _____

   (e.g., single, married, separated, divorced, widowed)

4. In what province of China were you born?

   _____

5. Where did you spend most of your childhood in China? (circle one)

   a. city   b. countryside

6. When did you leave China?

   _____

Child Culture

7. When you were a girl, what was your favorite game or toy?

   _____

8. As a child, who was your primary caregiver?

   _____

   (insert mother, grandmother, aunt, or other caregiver)

9. How many siblings did you have?
   Sisters:☐(specify number) Brothers:☐(specify number)

10. As a girl, who was your role model, and why?

    _____

    _____

11. What was the most important piece of advice your primary caregiver gave you?

    _____

    _____

12. How many children do you have?
    Daughters:☐(specify number) Sons:☐(specify number)

13. How many children do/did you want?
    Daughters:☐(specify number) Sons:☐(specify number)

14. When you were a girl, what profession did you dream of having?

    _____

15. What was your main job in China?

    _____

16. What is your main job in Canada?

    _____

17. Who do you think does most of the childrearing in typical Chinese families today? Using numbers 1–6, rank each of the following (with 1 representing most of the childrearing and 6 representing the least):

    Mother: ☐
    Father: ☐
    Grandparents: ☐
    Aunt/Uncle: ☐
    Daycare: ☐
    Nanny: ☐
    Other: ☐

Adoption Issues

18. In China, as elsewhere, babies are abandoned for a number of reasons. For each of the following reasons, circle what you think is most appropriate:

		Less important			More important	
a.	Poverty	1	2	3	4	5
b.	Birth Permission Papers	1	2	3	4	5
c.	Son preference	1	2	3	4	5
d.	Unmarried	1	2	3	4	5
e.	Poor education	1	2	3	4	5
f.	No support from father/family	1	2	3	4	5
g.	Regulation of family planning	1	2	3	4	5
h.	Abortion not available	1	2	3	4	5
i.	Abortion not desired	1	2	3	4	5
j.	Child disabled/health problem	1	2	3	4	5
k.	Better life for baby	1	2	3	4	5
l.	Disabled parent	1	2	3	4	5
m.	Other: (specify)	1	2	3	4	5

Comments:

_____

_____

19. Were you aware of the issue of child abandonment when you lived in China? How did you become aware? (choose one or more)

   a.   Was not aware

   b.   Newspaper

   c.   TV/Radio

    d.   Word of mouth

    e.   Other: (specify)

        If d. or e., please provide specifics:

_____

20.   There are many Children's Welfare Institutes in China. In your view, what is the most common background of the babies and children in these institutes?

		Less common			More common	
a.	Peasant	1	2	3	4	5
b.	Worker	1	2	3	4	5
c.	White collar	1	2	3	4	5
d.	Government employee	1	2	3	4	5
e.	Intellectual	1	2	3	4	5
f.	High ranking cadre	1	2	3	4	5
g.	Other: (specify)	1	2	3	4	5

    Comments:

_____

_____

21.   China has undergone immense economic and social changes in the last twenty years. Please describe any changes you have observed regarding the preference for boys over girls.

_____

_____

_____

_____

22. Assuming adopted girls should grow up with an understanding of China, how would you rate the importance of each of the following:

		Less important			More important	
a.	Visit original Child Welfare Institute	1	2	3	4	5
b.	Visit China	1	2	3	4	5
c.	Work/live in China for some time	1	2	3	4	5
d.	Speak Chinese	1	2	3	4	5
e.	Write Chinese	1	2	3	4	5
f.	Read Chinese	1	2	3	4	5
g.	Learn Chinese history	1	2	3	4	5
h.	Join local Chinese associations	1	2	3	4	5
i	Learn about Chinese culture: art, music, literature	1	2	3	4	5
j.	Observe Chinese holiday traditions	1	2	3	4	5
k.	Follow currents events in China	1	2	3	4	5
l.	Other: (specify)	1	2	3	4	5

Comments:

_____

_____

24. If an adopted girl has a chance to visit China as an adult, what places of cultural importance do you think she should see?

_____

_____

25. What advice would you give to children adopted from China?

_____

_____

26. What advice would you give to Canadian parents who have adopted from China?

_____

_____

_____

27. Can you recommend a book, a film, music, or artwork for parents who have adopted from China?

_____

28. Can you recommend a book, a film, music, or artwork for children adopted from China?

_____

Please feel free to share any other thoughts you have on the issues raised above.

_____

_____

_____

_____

On behalf of all the parents who will learn from your ideas, thank you very much.

Contributors

Jasmine Akbarali is a commercial litigator at Lerners LLP, a former Supreme Court of Canada law clerk, and gold medallist of her law class. She is a volunteer board member of the George Hull Centre for Children and Families, a children's mental health center in Toronto. Jasmine has a Pakistani father, a Finnish mother, Japanese cousins, and nieces who claim Italian, French-Canadian, Aboriginal, Jewish, and Newfoundlander heritage. She and her Canadian husband adopted Chinese twins, Maija and Eeva, from Guangxi Zhuang Autonomous Region in 2003. Blond, blue-eyed Lukas was born in 2005. When out together, they like to pretend they are a committee of the United Nations.

Jasmine Bent arrived in Canada when she was thirteen months old. Now fifteen, Jasmine has two younger sisters who are also adopted from China. Jasmine has a busy life; she belongs to biathalon and volleyball teams and has just started kickboxing classes. Modeling since she was four years old, Jasmine is currently preparing for roles in two upcoming short films being shot this summer in Ottawa. Her career goals lean toward journalism or law.

Cindy Boates is a Toronto-based management consultant. In her other life, she is the current president of the Toronto chapter of Families with Children from China, a support organization for families who have adopted from China. She is also their newsletter editor and co-moderator of an e-mail group focusing on homeland travel to China. She has both lived in Asia and traveled extensively there. But most important, she is mom to Sophie, adopted in 1998 and Lucy, adopted in 2002.

Lia Calderone was born on June 24, 1991, in Hunan province. Her parents, Peter and Lidia, adopted her in October 1991. In May 1995, Lia and her parents went back to Hunan to adopt another girl. They remained in China for two years. Lia lives in Montreal and attends Royal West Academy. She loves to spend time with her friends, read, listen to music, go to movies, and shop. Her favorite sport is karate and she has earned her black belt. Lia is leaning toward being a sports physical therapist, having her own *dojo,* and, if she has some spare time, doing martial arts stunts in the film industry.

Julie Chan is a management consultant and works for a major consulting firm managing large projects for her clients. Thomson Carswell is the publisher of her two business books and a newsletter where she is a regular columnist. Julie gained a national award for her work in *The Lawyers Weekly.* While she is a prolific business writer, this is her first but, with luck, not her last non-business publication. With a husband who is also a published author, her two daughters, at the ages four and six, are already writing and illustrating their own books.

Denise Davy is an award-winning reporter and columnist who has worked at the *Hamilton Spectator* covering social issues and women's issues for the past twenty years. In 1993 and 1995 Denise traveled to Southeast Asia on a journalism fellowship where she researched the lives of women and children. In 1995 she covered the United Nations Women's Conference in Beijing before traveling to India where she studied the country's family planning programs. She returned to China in 2000 to adopt Emma and then traveled back in 2004 to adopt Katie. Emma is the author of *China in My Heart*, in which she writes about her adoption journey.

Sarah Giddens is a Toronto-based educator and writer who has lived and worked in Africa, Hong Kong, and China. She might return to doctoral studies, but for now prefers to teach, learn Mandarin, and be with her family. Her work has been broadcast on CBC Radio and published in the *Globe and Mail*, *Chatelaine*, and *Today's Parent*.

Havard Gould is an award-winning reporter for CBC's *The National*. Born in Montreal, he has lived in or reported from almost everywhere in Canada. He now has a home in Toronto with his wife Helena, their three children, and one canoe.

Heidi Hatch was born in a small town in Derbyshire, England. Hitchhiking her way around Canada when she was twenty, Hatch was offered a job, and never returned to England. As a counsellor in a women's shelter, Hatch assists women through their journey of recovery from abusive relationships. She and her husband Bob adopted Chloe in 2000 from Anhui province and Meiling in 2004 from Hainan province. They live in the country, on a dirt road, with a pug dog, two Arabian horses, and a pony. She has been interested in all things Chinese since she was six years old when she told her family that she was running away from home and going to China on a donkey.

Patricia Hluchy is a features editor at the *Toronto Star* and former assistant managing editor at *Maclean's*, where she focused on the magazine's arts and lifestyle coverage. Her favorite ways to spend free time include hanging out with her daughter, Zhi, reading fiction, experiencing the natural world, and listening to lugubrious music by Slavic composers.

Douglas Hood has been on the faculties of Yale and Quinnipiac universities for twenty years. His stories have appeared in the collections *A Passage to the Heart* and *A Love Like No Other*, as well as in literary journals such as *Cimarron Review*. His children's book, *The Stone Hat*, is about China's terra-cotta warriors. He claims the unofficial world record for performing spinal taps, at more than 6,000. His daughter Suki is sixteen.

Tess Kalinowski is a reporter at the *Toronto Star* and a former assistant managing editor of the *London Free Press*. In 2000 she adopted her daughter Olivia. In June 2002 they welcomed the arrival of Olivia's cousin Claire from Hunan province.

Margaret Lawson is a pediatric endocrinologist at the Children's Hospital of Eastern Ontario and Associate Professor of Pediatrics at the University of Ottawa. Dr. Lawson is also the volunteer medical consultant for The Children's Bridge, the largest international adoption agency in Canada. She has written two book chapters and numerous articles about pediatric diabetes and endocrinology, as well as topics of interest to parents of children adopted internationally. Margaret and her husband Jonathan are the proud parents of Sophie and Isabella, both from Hunan province.

Glen McGregor is the former associate editor of *Frank* magazine and now works as a national affairs reporter with the *Ottawa Citizen*. He is father to two girls from Hunan province and has made several trips back to China since their adoptions. He is learning, slowly, to speak Mandarin and is clinically addicted to dim sum.

Lilian Nattel lives in Toronto with her husband and two daughters. She is the author of *The Singing Fire* (Knopf Toronto/Scribner NY, 2004) and *The River Midnight* (Knopf Toronto/Scribner NY, 1999). She is currently immersed in another novel. Her family is hoping to visit China in the not too distant future, but in the meantime content themselves with getting to know the different regions of Canada.

Susan Olding's poetry and essays have appeared in literary journals and anthologies throughout Canada and the United States. She's a two-time winner of the Event Creative Non-fiction contest and her writing has been shortlisted for a CBC Literary Award, two Western Magazine Awards, and a National Magazine Award. A contributor to EMK's *Adoption Parenting: Creating a Toolbox, Building Connections*, she has also presented workshops on adoption-related topics. She lives with her family in Kingston, Ontario, where she teaches at the Writing Centre and with the Department of Film and Media at Queen's University.

Shelley Page is a feature writer and columnist at the *Ottawa Citizen* and two-time winner of a National Newspaper Award. In 2007 she won the award for best piece of investigative newspaper reporting in Canada. Her writing on adoption issues has appeared in many newspapers, as well as in *Adoptive Families* and *Today's Parent* magazines. She is a director of the Children's Bridge Foundation, which supports orphans in China and elsewhere. She is mom to two spicy Hunan girls.

Ann Rauhala is a former columnist and foreign editor of the *Globe and Mail*, now director of newspapers at the School of Journalism at Ryerson University in Toronto. Ann isn't very good at sewing dragon dance costumes or cooking Chinese dumplings, but she did want her daughter to know how important her arrival was to her family. This collection is that keepsake.

Sonja Smits is an award-winning actress who lives in Toronto. She has had the good luck to star in three television series as well as numerous feature films and on stage. She has had the even better luck to be the mother of two children, a daughter adopted from Western Canada and a son adopted from China.

Evan Solomon is the Gemini-winning host of CBC News *Sunday Night* and host of CBC Newsworld's weekly program about print culture called *HotType*. Passionate about issues of technology, social change, and culture, Solomon was the creator and editor-in-chief of the award-winning *Shift* magazine, and co-founder of the Ingenuity Project, which focuses on finding practical solutions to sustainable development. He is the author of several books including *Crossing the Distance*, and a children's book, *Nathaniel McDaniel and the Magic Attic: Bigbread's Hook*. He lives in Toronto with his wife, son, and daughter.

Steve Whan lives in North Vancouver, B.C., with his wife and two daughters. Realizing there was a lack of stories with a Chinese heroine to read to his daughters, Steve wrote his own.

Jan Wong is a Canadian journalist, internationally known author, and former Beijing bureau chief for the *Globe and Mail* newspaper. She is author of *Red China Blues*, *Jan Wong's China*, and *Beijing Confidential* and lives with her family in Toronto, where she is a reporter for the *Globe and Mail*.

Acknowledgments

My gratitude, first, to the contributors for sharing their personal lives and donating their writing — all with patience and good humor.

For her creativity and sensitivity as a research assistant, thank you to Lindsay Mattick. For their encouragement and advice, my thanks to Julie Chan, Darlene Varaleau, and Natasha Rudnick. For her insightful photography, thanks to Catherine Farquharson. For their editing acumen, thanks to Helena Moncrieff and Joyce Grant.

For valuable assistance and suggestions along the way, thank you to an astonishing network of parents: in particular, Catherine Bickley, Jennifer Dawson, Alexandra Rowland, Susan Bishop, Stephen Brunt, Mary Child, and Brian Boyd.

Thank you to my friends and colleagues in the School of Journalism at Ryerson University, especially Don Gibb and Joyce Smith, for their support. I'm grateful also to the Dean's Office of the Faculty of Communication and Design, in particular Irene Devine and Ira Levine, for financial assistance.

I must thank Jen Hale and the staff at ECW who have been unfailingly kind and astute.

Thank you to my mother and father and to Lorne, Sam, and Annie.

Finally, thank you to the woman we have never met who gave birth to Annie. You would be proud.